D0974837

Locked In Locked Out

by

Shawn Jennings, MD

To Anna

With Love

Shawn

DREAMCATCHER PUBLISHING
Saint John • New Brunswick • Canada

Copyright © 2002 Shawn Jennings

First Printing - August 2002
Second Printing - November 2002
Third Printing - February 2003

All rights reserved. No part of this publication may be reproduced or transmitted in any form or by any means – electronic or mechanical, including photocopying, recording or any information storage and retrieval system – without written permission from the Publisher, except by a reviewer who wishes to quote brief passages for inclusion in a review.

Disclaimer:
Patient names in this book are fictional to protect patient confidentiality, except Pauli, Art and Hilda, and Barbara. All names of therapists, nurses, doctors, and friends are actual names, unless otherwise indicated.

Canadian Cataloguing in Publication Data

Jennings, Shawn - 1953

Locked In Locked Out

ISBN - 1-894372-23-9
        1. Jennings, Shawn--Health. 2. Cerebrovascular disease--Patients--Canada–
Biography. I. Title
        RC388.5.J45 2002   362.1'9681'0092   C2002-903618-6

Editor: Yvonne Wilson

Typesetter: Chas Goguen

Cover Photo: Colin Jennings

Cover Design: Dawn Drew, INK Graphic Design Services Corp.

Printed and bound in Canada

DREAMCATCHER PUBLISHING INC.
1 Market Square
Suite 306 Dockside
Saint John, New Brunswick, Canada E2L 4Z6
www.dreamcatcher.nb.ca

This book is dedicated to my wife Jill, whose love
sustained me and lighted my way.

FOREWORD

I have known Shawn Jennings for over twenty years as a colleague, business partner and friend.

Shawn came to practice medicine soon after I arrived back in Saint John. He took over a large practice from a well loved physician, Dr. Norbert Grant. Practices seem to age with the physician, so Shawn was taking over an elderly and therefore time-consuming and challenging practice. Eventually we both ended up participating in building a new medical clinic and formed a sign-out group where we covered one another's practices on evenings and weekends.

Every time I covered Shawn I always thought: "How does he do it?" He had twice as many people in hospital as I did. They all seemed to be just shy of a hundred years old and had multiple problems. Not only that but they all loved him.

Many doctors are respected, some are revered, a few are loved. Shawn was one of the latter. You could tell by the way people talked about him that he was a cherished "member of the family".

Really good family doctors almost make their practices like a big family and of course become like part of their patients' families. Shawn was that kind of physician. I took over some of his patients after his stroke. They still ask about him or tell me about their contacts with him with the same warmth and affection they felt for him when he was tending to their needs.

Shawn's stroke was a shock to the medical and hospital community. In his book he says he was not a leader in the medical community but he was something more, he was an example. He was an example of what a dedicated, conscientious, caring physician is and should be. Shawn did the house-call, nursing home visits, counseling and in a hundred different ways showed he cared for his patients. They reciprocated and showed they cared for him.

Shawn's stroke and his subsequent fight to regain a life for himself has been an inspiration to many. Although I have witnessed much strength and courage as a physician, I can think of few more stirring examples than Shawn's. I personally have had to ask myself, if I were faced with the challenges he has met and overcome, would I have had the courage and strength to carry on as he has done.

Shawn was well loved by the nurses and hospital staff as well as his patients. One nurse said to me after his stroke: "I just can't imagine not hearing his laugh again. We could always hear him laughing before he even got on the ward." Recently she told me she had seen him again and said: "You know his laugh still sounds the same."

Shawn says in his book: "I didn't have to find humor, humor just found me." It wasn't just humor. It was joy.

Shawn's answer to life is love. He showed it before his stroke and he continues to do so after. He was before and is now what we all should be – a loving and joyful person who faces life's difficulties and does his best to deal with them.

- Dr. Stephen Willis
Saint John Medical Clinic

The author would like to acknowledge the Allergan Corporation, the makers of Botox, for their kindness and their support in this project.

ACKNOWLEDGEMENTS

These acknowledgements pertain only to the making of this book; they do not refer to the people responsible in my rehabilitation – the doctors, nurses, therapists, friends, and relatives. These I have previously thanked, and to them I am forever indebted.

First I have to thank my readers for their encouragement, suggestions, and reviews: Dr. Peter Bailey, Patti Nicholson, Heather Erb, Claire McIlveen, and many family members.

A special 'thank you' to Ron Harris, who wrote 'About the Book' and to Dr. Stephen Willis who wrote the foreword; both humbled me by their gracious words; and finally Rick Hanson, who commands not only my admiration but the world's.

The people at DreamCatcher Publishing, Inc.: Elizabeth Margaris – the publisher and Yvonne Wilson – the editor. I thank them for their positive energy, encouragement, and suggestions.

Finally, a warm thanks to Allergan Pharmaceuticals for their sponsorship in the publication of this book.

ABOUT THE BOOK

The shy, engaging Shawn and his alter ego Dr. Jennings, have written an intimate story of how courage and determination can transcend trauma and disability. Shawn tells us about the bewilderment, fear, physical and emotional disruption that a brainstem stroke causes. It engulfs its victim in a tumult of thoughts and feelings and it robs them of the power to convey the effects of this turmoil to family and other helpers. Shawn's story takes us on a journey through the hard work of rehabilitation and shows how memory and past experiences are, at once, bittersweet yet valuable to progress. At the same time Dr. Jennings, the family practitioner, reflects on all these experiences in the context of his own practice as a physician and towards himself as a patient. He describes the relationship between patient and rehabilitation professional and highlights the special qualities these dedicated people have. In a special twist to his story, Shawn talks about his shyness, of an earlier bout with depression and of social anxiety and panic attacks. These are all states in which persons strive to assert control of feelings or circumstances over which they perceive they have little or no influence. Here is a theme within a theme as Shawn tries to regain power over the seemingly insurmountable sequelae of the stroke and it provides a context for Shawn's personal reaffirmation of, for him, the power of love and faith.

Shawn and Dr. Jennings meld together as husband, father, doctor, patient, stroke victim to be the warm, modest, humorous, caring person so clearly evident in his story. It will most assuredly have important meaning for people who have suffered brainstem stroke but has a much wider relevance for all people who wish to understand what happens to those whose lives are so suddenly changed by traumatic events. I think it is required reading for all of us who practice in the world of physical rehabilitation and an eye-opener for all.

- Ron Harris, Ph.D., L.Psych.
Administrative Director,
Stan Cassidy Centre for Rehabilitation
Fredericton, NB

AUTHOR'S FOREWORD

Patti Nicholson has been an important person in my life. She is a nurse whom I had the pleasure of working with on various committees before my illness. She was the first person to put the idea of writing a book in my head.

I have suffered a unique type of stroke involving the brainstem. The brainstem is the canal through which all the messages from the brain are sent to the rest of the body. A stroke in this area is particularly devastating. A cerebral stroke is the common type of stroke: it involves one side of the body and may affect speech and swallowing. The brainstem stroke usually affects both sides of the body, and usually always, the speech and swallowing activities. The facial muscles are paralyzed, leaving only eyelid movement. Even the extraocular muscles are involved, leaving survivors with double vision. The brain is left perfectly intact, meaning that there is no confusion or personality change. The survivor is left imprisoned inside a body with no movement.

I found myself in this state – aptly called the Locked In Syndrome – in May of 1999.

Patti helped my wife and me in many ways during my convalescence, and it was she who encouraged me to write. But why would I? Who would care about what I went through?

I felt so alone when I was 'locked in'. I would have been reassured hearing about other brainstem stroke survivors, and how they felt. I later found books on the subject written by other survivors, but in one book the survivor dies soon after the book is published; in another, the survivor has a second stroke after surviving the first stroke. They may not be good reading for the survivors early in their illness.

Maybe it will be interesting reading coming from a doctor's

perspective – as former caregiver and now patient. I have never been a patient before. I never had an intravenous or been washed by someone or been constipated. New adventures.

I hope this book will be of some small comfort to a new survivor somewhere, sometime. If I do that then I've succeeded. I know how the new survivor feels: alone, like you are the only one to have ever gone through this. But you're not alone, a few of us have 'been there – done that'. I hope my thoughts may sound familiar to you, and you say, "Yeah, that's what I thought!" I really do want you to know: you are not alone.

I hope this book gives you some hope. I hope you work hard. I hope your dream of recovery comes true but if it doesn't, I hope you can accept reality also: life has changed for you. Dreams have been broken; your focus in life may have to be altered, but it is worth it. Life is worth it. Be happy to have gotten this far, to be a survivor and able to have these words read to you. Be patient and let's see how far you go.

To the rest of my able-bodied readers, if you attempt to read this, I will add a lot of personal reflections, so it may be interesting for you too. I may even add some romance and sex!

I will try not to talk like a doctor but that may be impossible. If I do – I'm sorry.

This may never be published – I'm not a writer and I have no illusions that I am – but it will be a fun project for me – something to do other than exercise and good therapy for my mind.

I wrote most of this account in my mind, as I lay 'locked in'. I could not move, so typing was impossible. I could have dictated via my eye movements to Jill, but this would have been too time consuming and frustrating. It was hard enough trying to communicate my basic needs. I suppose planning this book while 'locked in' helped keep me sane.

I started typing once I could move my left hand, so the writing of this book became therapeutic for my hand – a secondary gain. I wrote this account by using one hand and patience.

I started Christmas of 1999 and finished around Christmas of 2001. I have Jill's parents, Dr. Bill and Adele Moreside, to thank for supplying me with a laptop so I could start putting down my thoughts.

The priority was my rehabilitation; writing this book was a needed distraction. It took time – two hours grabbed when I could – not necessarily every day. I felt guilty taking time off from my exercises to write, but you need some distraction – you can't work all the time.

My children, Colin, Beth, and Tara have shown me strength and courage. My wife and I had little to worry about at home. In what surely must have been a scary situation for them, they showed us independence far beyond their years. I am indebted and overwhelmed by their care and love for me.

I could not have gone through this without the love and caring of my wife. It was she who stayed by my side from day one. It was she whom I cried with. It was she who wiped my nose, suctioned out my trachea, yet gently wiped my brow. It was she who lifted my spirits, by a simple smile, yet it was she who cajoled me into trying harder in my long months of rehabilitation. It was her love that made me realize what life was all about. It was her love that sustained me throughout this crisis in my life. This book is a small product of that love. I love you, Jill, and this book is dedicated to you.

CHAPTER 1 – THE EVENT

May 13th, 1999 was bright and promising, or so I thought. The smell of new grass was in the air. It was the type of day you waited all winter to feel. I got up and had a shower, not knowing that it would be the last time I would have a shower for months. I packed my golf clothes in my sports bag and headed downstairs. I ate my regular cereal while I marveled at the glorious day that awaited me. I talked to Jenny, my dog, and then climbed into my truck without a care and without a thought about what I would soon consider a dream – the ability to drive. Soon I was heading down the highway for the hospital.

I am a family physician who has been in practice for twenty years. I enjoyed my life. I took pleasure in the patient – doctor interaction and liked the variety of complaints that a family physician sees. The one thing I never enjoyed was the constant time-stress that was the nature of this work. There was always the balance of giving enough time to each patient and the demand to see everyone who wanted to be seen. After twenty years, I think I molded my practice to fit my personality.

This was to be a special day. I was taking the afternoon off for a golf game. An afternoon with no phone calls, no thinking about diagnoses, no questions to answer, nothing but an easy banter with my buddies and a nice walk on a pleasant day. The golf itself was secondary to the social interaction and the surroundings.

With this on my mind I headed into the hospital. I made my rounds without incident. Everyone was doing as expected. One of the last patients I saw was Pauli, an unfortunate lady in her early sixties who had Scleroderma, a progressive disease that would be soon entering the terminal stages for her. She had been a well lady, looking less than her chronological age, until about five years previous when this insidious disease started. It had progressed at an alarming rate. At first it caused her skin on her hands to tighten, to the extent her fingers were unable to bend and the skin had split open over the knuckles, leaving open sores that wouldn't heal. Then the skin around her mouth tightened in such a way that it caused a loss of expression and difficulty with speech. Her legs became involved, making walking impossible. Next it started to work its way into her digestive system, stealing her ability to swallow or digest food, leaving her with a malabsorption syndrome and chronic diarrhea. Lately, we had to insert a gastrotomy tube into her stomach to give her nutrition. This bypasses the mouth and esophagus enabling us to give a liquid supplement. I had been torn by this decision to give her supplementation, as it would prolong the inevitable. I was sure what life remained to her would be filled with pain, suffering, and of poor quality, but she made my decision easy, as it was her wish to keep going. Finally, in what I considered was going to be the final straw, her kidneys started to be involved.

To complicate things further, she had a stroke as a consequence of the disease involving her blood vessels. Besides the paralysis she was aphasic, hampering her ability to communicate verbally.

Scleroderma, also known as Progressive Systemic Sclerosis is caused by too much collagen being laid down in the tissues causing a fibrosis or stiffness in the body part. The skin loses its elasticity and normal cells are being displaced. The cause of this phenomenon happening is unknown.

Her family had been very supportive. Her husband had kept her at home as long as he could until the diarrhea, immobility, and other factors led him and me to her admission. She had just gone from an active ward to this chronic care ward when I went to see her this day. She would be the last patient I would see.

"Good morning, Pauli," I said.

"Aaaa," she responded as best she could.

"Did you have a good night?"

"Mmmmm, Au ha soo diaea," she tried to say.

"Some diarrhea?" I guessed.

"Aaaa"

"Did you take the MCT oil with your meal last night?" (This is a substitute for butter or margarine that is easy to digest.)

"Ugh!" she grimaced.

"Well, I'll have to look at your chart to see if there are any meds that maybe we should look at. What did they give you to eat last night?" I knew this was a foolish question to ask as soon as I said it; how could she respond?

"Sorry!" I said sheepishly. She chuckled.

"I'll ask the nurse." I proceeded to examine her hands, which were grossly contracted like a bird's claw and just as delicate. Her mouth was drawn back exposing her upper teeth, but she could still smile as she was doing now. I carefully lifted up her pajama top, exposing her upper abdomen so I could see her gastrotomy tube, which was placed in the week before. It looked to be healing just fine, despite the Scleroderma.

"Be good!" I said. She nodded and I strolled away and examined the chart. After I wrote my progress notes and typed in my orders into the computer, I left the floor. I left the hospital quite quickly and jumped into my truck. Rolling down the windows, I breathed in the fresh air – no air conditioning for me today. I looked out to the harbour at the clear blue sea, as I neared my office, and once again marveled at the day. Just the morning to get through and I would be free. I drove into the parking lot at my clinic and turned my head around to back up. It was approximately 9 o'clock.

As I turned my head, a peculiar sensation hit me: my vision started to move backwards and forwards. A ringing sensation developed in my head.

Vertigo! I thought. The McDonald's sign across the street moved back and forth.

I noticed a man sitting in his car beside me. *Hope I don't make a fool of myself!*

I was due to start in the office now. I felt I couldn't walk so I phoned my wife on the cellular, who functions as a nurse in my office. She usually doesn't work on Thursdays and she later told me that I was double lucky, as there was no battery life left on the phone after my call.

My receptionist answered the phone and I asked to speak to Jill. " I won't be able to make it in. I'm awful dizzy!"

"Where are you?" she said, alarmed at the concern in my voice.

"In the upper parking lot."

I don't remember much about the next few minutes until I saw Jill in front of my truck. She found me with the door open and my seatbelt unfastened. I don't remember doing this but I vaguely recall feeling hot, so I may have opened the door for air.

I again reiterated that I was dizzy. She felt that I should go to the hospital, so helped me out of the car. I staggered over to the back seat of her car, which I had just happened to park beside. I had great difficulty in arranging myself to get in a comfortable position. I thought this was a real good attack of vertigo. Jill drove around to the other side of the building to tell my receptionist and my patients who had already arrived what she was doing.

While she was gone, I realized I was going in and out of consciousness. I also had an idea that this was more than vertigo. My right hand was feeling heavy and numb. I became aware that my breathing was laboured. My lips were pouting and I could almost hear myself snore. I felt I should stop this, straighten up, but weariness overcame me. Sleep would feel so good.

Jill was gone but seconds. When she returned, she was alarmed at my condition. I could hear her asking me questions. I wanted to respond, to tell her about my hand, to tell her what I suspected was happening to me, but nothing would come out. When

I tried to speak, all that came out was a garbled, "mmmm". As she drove away to the hospital, I became more unconscious. As if in a dream, I could hear her imploring me to keep talking and keep awake. My response to her was a deep groan or a snore.

My final sense of awareness was in front of the Emergency Dept. I saw and felt a male nurse and an orderly, both of whom I knew, lift me out of the car. I heard someone say, "We just saw him this morning!" That was the last thing I heard, as I lapsed into that sleep I seemed to so desperately need.

CHAPTER 2 – THE DIAGNOSIS

I was in deep, deep trouble and I was the only one who knew. I knew I was having a stroke and I couldn't tell them – I was in bye-bye land. After examinations and blood tests, they had ruled out the most common causes of sudden loss of consciousness and sent me for a CT scan. Unfortunately it was read as negative, not through an error in judgment but poor quality. I was having sonorous respirations causing my head to move and thus the unfortunate picture. However even if the picture had been perfect, there is a likely chance that the diagnosis would have eluded them at this point.

More time was spent waiting for some clinical change; as it turned out, time I could ill afford. Based on the results of the CT scan, it would appear that no major event had occurred in my brain to cause this sudden loss of consciousness. Dr. Vaillencourt, the emergentologist, was perplexed. At first, he was relieved that the CT scan had shown no tumor or blood in my brain, and he entertained the possibility I had had a seizure and was now in my post-seizure state. He was waiting for me to arouse, but I remained somnolent.

My wife was becoming frantic; when she was told there was a lot of distortion on the first film, she knew I hadn't had a seizure, so she implored them to do another CT scan. They did, but I had to be returned because the sonorous respirations were worse. Another CT scan under those conditions would have been a waste of time. They recommended intubation.

About this time, Dr. Sandy McDougall, a former classmate of mine and the neurologist on call that day, examined me and was concerned I was 'locked in'.

To intubate, a medication is given to paralyze muscles, a hollow tube with a balloon on one end is inserted down the throat and into the larynx or windpipe. Some people have anatomy that makes this hard to do. I was one of these people. An anesthetist had to be called down to try the intubation, after a few failed attempts by the emergentologists. The significance of this was that I ended up with aspiration pneumonia. Oral secretions laden with bacteria cause this by passing into the lungs. Coughing normally prevents this, but being unconscious, this defensive mechanism was absent, and the oral secretions may settle into the lungs undisturbed.

They were now breathing for me by pumping a bag attached to my intubation tube. After I was sent back for another CT scan, something was seen. I appeared to have a clot in my left vertebral artery. No blood was flowing to my brainstem. I was having a brainstem stroke.

A stroke usually happens when a clot interrupts the normal blood flow. The clot forms in a narrowed vessel that has had its canal reduced by cholesterol plaque. A clot forms here and either occludes the vessel at this point or flies off and occludes another smaller vessel distally. This same scenario happens in heart attacks. Actually they are both called infarcts, and strokes are often now called brain attacks.

Cells need blood-carrying oxygen to live; without blood, they quickly die. It was now after 12 pm and my stroke had started at 9 am. Time is critical: the more time that has elapsed – the more cellular death.

The brainstem looks after very primitive functions such as sleeping, eating, breathing and heart rate; functions necessary for even the lowest creatures in the evolutionary chain. Also, all the commands from the brain to the rest of the body pass through here. Thus a stroke in this area usually causes paralysis to both sides of the body. A patient can't breathe properly, cannot swallow, cannot speak, and often has double vision. The eyelids are the only part of the anatomy able to move. Most brainstem strokes don't survive. Of those that do survive, most stay significantly impaired. A few stay 'locked in' – surviving with a normal functioning brain but being unable to move, swallow, or talk. Most survivors of a brainstem stroke go through a 'locked in' phase and improve. A very small percentage of patients recover completely.

Some damage to the brainstem must have already occurred. To leave me as I was would probably mean death. Dr. John Whelan, a radiologist, attempted a cerebral angiography to dissolve the clot. This is a procedure whereby an incision is made in the groin and a small tube is run up the femoral artery to the aorta and then up to the vertebral artery, in the back of the neck. Dr. Whelan decided to call in Dr. Robert MacDonald, an interventional cardiologist, to help. Dr. MacDonald also happens to be an old classmate of mine from medical school.

Together they attempted the procedure and ran into problems: my left vertebral artery bled after they injected it with TPA. The clot had formed from a tear on the artery and dissolving the clot caused bleeding.

Now they had a real problem. If they continued the drug, I would bleed to death. To leave me as I was would be probable death. So they gave me enough TPA to open a small canal through the clot; but had to stop, when the vessel started to bleed profusely.

A clot would quickly plug up this lumen, so it had to be maintained. Heparin is a drug that we use to prevent clots and to dissolve them, although in a much slower fashion than TPA. They gave me this via an intravenous, in hope that it would prevent the lumen from closing up and dissolve the clot at the same time. Heparin could cause the artery to bleed more but my chances were better with Heparin than without. So in this precarious state, I was sent to the NICU or Neurological Intensive Care Unit under the care of Dr. Peter Bailey.

I am indebted to all the above doctors for my life.

Meanwhile, Dr. Barry, the department head of Radiology, had taken my wife to his office to explain the diagnosis, and angiography. He let her stay in his office for the afternoon. My mother,

Doreen McLaughlin, joined her at this point. When he returned some time later, he didn't have good news. He thought Jill should probably call in my children to see me.

* * *

Two weeks prior to this stroke I was involved in a near automobile collision. I had just finished some minor surgery at St. Joseph's Hospital and was heading to the Saint John Regional Hospital. As I entered an intersection, a blue Ford F-150 turned in front of me. I was about to hit it broadside. I have never been involved in an automobile accident, but I was sure this was it. There was a girl in the front passenger seat and our eyes met. I thought I was about to slam into her. As I prayed, *Dear God- No!* I slammed on the brakes and somehow missed the pick-up by mere inches. The woman was oblivious to the danger and never altered her speed. I came to a screeching halt. A man in a vehicle, who saw the whole event, to my right, shook his head.

Later that morning, I felt a vague ache in my neck while making rounds at the hospital. At noon I had lunch with a friend of mine, Harry Colwell, and experienced a strange warm sensation in my neck that made me a little faint. I didn't say anything to my companion but just continued nibbling at my lunch. I expect that was the moment my blood vessel bled. On leaving the lunch, I felt a little wobbly on my feet but thought nothing of it.

The ache intensified that afternoon in the office. I realized I had a whiplash (or so I thought). I always wondered what one felt like. I have treated many patients with this malady over the years, so it was interesting to actually experience one. Some of them can become quite chronic; the majority of them are minor. I was sure mine would prove to be mild. I took some Advil and finished up my day.

Later that night and throughout the week I used Advil and

occasionally put wet heat on my neck. I was not concerned. I continued to run my office, oversee my patients in hospital, and do my chores at home. My first golf game of the season was due and I thought the exercise might actually do the neck some good. Patients who have the best outcomes with whiplash are those who can ignore the pain and continue with normal activities. Sometimes the pain is too intense to ignore, leading to fear of bending the neck and subsequently ending up with chronic, stiff, painful necks. I was determined not to be one of those.

It was about a week after my whiplash that my partner, Dr. Winston Lee, and I decided to tee off. My first hole of the year was a success; I had a par and hit the ball well. It will be the last hole, I play well – ever.

As I approached the second tee, I felt dizzy. My legs started to feel rubbery. *Funny,* I thought, *I ate my lunch, but I feel somewhat hypoglycemic* (low blood sugar).

Somehow I hit a perfect drive down the middle of the fairway. My partner hit one into the rough. What was his excuse! As we walked up the fairway, we talked easily, but I still felt very shaky. I had still not told him how I felt. I prayed he would find his ball because I didn't want to walk over. He did, and as I stood over my ball, my legs felt weak, my head was dizzy, my mouth was dry, and I felt somewhat nauseous. I hit the ball more from muscle memory than from skill and landed the ball just off the green.

I putted quickly in two strokes, not really caring about the outcome. On our way to the third hole, we walked down a little hill. I really wasn't sure if I would make it. "Winston, I'm feeling a bit woozy. I'm dizzy, sort of weak in the knees. Everything's going around," I said, as I sat down on a bench. "You go ahead and hit."

He drove the ball up to an elevated green. I knew I couldn't continue as my turn came. "I can't do it, old boy. I don't think I can even walk back."

I noticed an approaching group behind us with golf carts.

When they had reached us, I asked if one of them would mind driving me back to my car.

I clambered on the golf cart holding my golf clubs precariously to my body and headed off. I was afraid I might vomit as the bumping and to and fro motion of the golf cart sent my head spinning. Arriving back at my truck, I somehow managed to get my clubs in back of the truck. After the ride, my head was really spinning and I had great difficulty keeping my feet. I held onto the truck and made my way into the passenger seat. I felt very weak and broke out into a sweat. I couldn't focus on the surrounding locale. I sat there waiting for Winston.

When he came, we decided to head to the Emergency Department, which was just down the road. I felt like a fool walking into Emergency with my golf shoes on and with Winston supporting me. After the nurses took the routine measurements, bloods, and history, Dr. Chris Vaillencourt, the same Emergentologist who would see me the day I had my stroke, came in. He took a history and examined me, finding fluid in my middle ear.

"Seems as though you have vertigo – probably caused by that fluid in your middle ear. I'm going to set you up with an IV and give you Maxeran. OK?"

I mentioned my whiplash injury. He and I couldn't fathom how that type of injury could give me these symptoms, so I agreed to his plan. But something was bothering me: I have always had fluid in my ears; it has been a chronic problem since I was a youngster, but it never caused vertigo. Yet I had to concede, if I were in Dr. Vaillencourt's shoes, I would make the same diagnosis. I didn't want to sound like a baby by saying, "But I always have fluid in my ears!"

After lying on the stretcher and receiving the IV Maxeran, the vertigo started to subside. My wife arrived and soon I was good enough to go home. I noted that my gait was wide-based which wasn't unusual considering the fact I just had a bout of vertigo.

Dr. Tees, an Otolaryngologist, agreed to see me the next

day. I'd seen him before with my chronic ear problems and he worked in the same medical clinic. He did a myringotomy – a procedure whereby the tympanic membrane or eardrum is lanced and the excess fluid from the middle ear is drained.

This was a Friday and that weekend I laid low. A patient phoned me at home that afternoon, complaining of severe pain in her leg. She was a diabetic and I feared she might be having an acute occlusion of her artery. I was in no condition to go to her and I told her to go immediately to the Emergency Department. I hated not being available for her, in her time of need, but it had to be. It would later turn out that it was an arterial occlusion; she would lose the leg.

That weekend I continued to apply heat to my aching neck and took the occasional Advil. My gait stayed unsteady but not remarkably so. I felt like I could work on Monday. At the hospital I met Dr. Sandy MacDougall – who would later be involved with me on the day of my stroke – and I told him my tale. I was not convinced it was my ears that caused the vertigo. He had a few minutes, so he took me to an exam room in the hospital.

I was surprised to find that I absolutely could not walk heel to toe. He felt things were not normal, and with the history of vertigo, gait disturbance and pain, I warranted a CT scan. His secretary would call me when that was booked. I expected it would be a week or two before this could be done, but I felt better knowing further investigation was going to be done.

That was a Monday and the stroke happened three days later. I have often wondered: what if I had complained more in the Emergency Dept.? I didn't believe the fluid caused the vertigo; would the results have been different? Did the fact that I was a physician being evaluated by a colleague prevent me from complaining? What if the CT scan had been done sooner? But it didn't seem like an emergency to me. I was walking around the hospital making rounds. What if the first CT scan was positive, or was that likely?

'What ifs?' – 'What ifs?' Always when something like this

happens, there are a lot of 'what ifs?' Some people get hung up on the 'what ifs?' when bad things happen. I found out early that you can 'what if?' all you like, but it won't change anything. Accept it and move on. Bad things happen.

*   *   *

I awoke that evening from my coma. My first conscious thought was, "My God, they have a catheter in my dink! This is serious!"

CHAPTER 3 – THE NEUROLOGICAL INTENSIVE CARE UNIT

When I awoke, I was aware of nurses hovering around me. I wanted to speak to them but I found myself unable to respond. *No wonder*, I thought, *they have put a tube in my throat.* I slowly became aware that I was intubated and on a respirator (a machine that breathes for you).

It did not concern me that I had been intubated. I was strangely comfortable with my situation. It was not long before Dr. Bailey came. I do not remember who it was but someone told me to blink once for 'yes' and twice for 'no'. This became my main mode of communication for months. Dr. Bailey explained that I had had a stroke and asked me if I understood. I blinked once. He then asked me simple questions to which I responded appropriately. He determined that I was thinking clearly and said so to the nurses around. I thought, *Of course I'm OK; I've had a little ministroke. Come on guys!*

Jill was at my side soon thereafter. She stroked my hair and patted my hand. The closeness and love I felt for this woman, at that moment, mingled with the warmth I received from the comatose state.

I had no near death experience that I can remember, but despite all that was done: the traumatic intubation, the angiogram, the catheterization, and the IV's, I awoke feeling great. I felt as though I had just had a good sleep. I felt as though something good had just happened. I really didn't want to wake up. Did I experience something? Was this just a normal physiological response after a coma? I don't know, but I'll never be afraid of a coma.

I was not at all concerned at what had befallen me. It didn't seem important. It was like waking up in your Grandma's home with a toasty, warm, puff wrapped around you; or a foggy morning with nothing to get up for so you curl up for a longer snooze. The respirator pushing air into my lungs, my inability to move, the IV's, all of these things which should have panicked me had no effect. I was calm.

As a doctor, I used to tell grieving or worried relatives who had loved ones in a coma from whatever cause, that they were not suffering. I said it without really knowing, but now I can say with conviction: they are not suffering. If you have a loved one with cancer or any terminal illness, who is going in and out of consciousness: they are not suffering. The coma is a state of mind that is restful. Welcome it.

Later in my rehabilitation I comforted a mourning mother who had lost her son. Her son, a young man of eighteen years of age, had a congenital heart condition that had run its course and required a heart transplant. Unfortunately the new heart he was given failed, and he lived for a number of days without a heart until a second heart was found. The second transplant was successful but the days of trying to keep him on the heart bypass machine took its toll, and he hemorrhaged. Unbeknownst to me, the mother was afraid he had suffered when he was comatose without a heart. I happened to mention that while in my coma I was very restful. I have no idea why I even mentioned this. The mother was shocked and, while crying, thanked me for giving her such a beautiful gift.

The next few hours and through the night were hazy. I remember seeing my children that evening or do I? I was restless that night, wanting to shift my body but it wouldn't respond. The next morning Dr. Bailey told me they were going to do another angiogram. The news elicited no fear, anxiety, or concern. I met the news with that same unconcerned attitude I felt about my whole situation. I must have been in a semi-comatose state because I remember only moments of the trip downstairs. I do not remember the procedure except I remember my colleagues squealing, "We got it! It's gone!"

What they were saying was that the clot had dissolved in the artery from the use of Heparin overnight. I would live, but in what condition? No one could say for sure at this point but Dr. Bailey took my family aside and explained to them, based on the damage seen on CT scan, what to expect.

"Your Dad is going to live but he will never be the same. His brain will be fine. He knows you and his personality will be the same as it always was. He won't be able to speak as well as before, but I think he can retrain his speech to a certain extent. I don't know how much he will get back in his arms and legs, but he probably won't walk. The injury affected his swallowing so we will have to perform a tracheostomy. Hopefully, in time, he will learn to swallow and this can come out. In the meantime, he will need tube feedings."

Dr. Bailey would later prove to be quite accurate in his assessment.

My wife and kids later told me they had no questions. They were trying to get used to the idea that I was critically ill. Their world had suddenly changed and yet there were no distinguishing features to mark today from yesterday. Events happen in everybody's life that change his or her life forever. My event had occurred.

Over the course of the next few days, my circumstance became more apparent to me. I had had a stroke but a most unusual one, a brainstem stroke. I searched my memory if I had ever seen one: No, in twenty years I had never come across this condition. I thought it couldn't be too bad; after all, I could feel. I could feel my toes, hands, face, everything. I seemed to have no sensory deficit.

In some ways, a deprivation of the senses would have been welcome. My limbs rebelled at not being able to move. I spent hours aching in different areas of my body. The nurses turned me every two hours – a relief from my agony – but in a few minutes the pain would start in some other area of my body. I was unable to scream out or make any commotion to signal anyone, so I had to be content

to wait until someone happened to come by. Then I would try to
make my distress apparent by batting my eyelashes furiously.

An anatomy lesson would proceed, "Is something the matter,
Shawn?"

One blink.
"Are you in pain?"
One blink.
"Is it your arm?"
Two blinks.
"Your head?"
Two blinks.
"Your legs?"
One blink.
"Is it your right leg?"
One blink.
"Is it your calf?"
One blink.

The nurse rectified the problem, which usually meant just
placing the leg in a different position. Sometimes there was more
than one pain and I soon learnt that trying to communicate about
multiple areas of the body only caused confusion. I decided that I
had to indicate which area hurt the worst and be content with some
relief.

The worst time was the night. The nurses, rightfully so, would
tend not to come around as often, so as not to disturb one's sleep. I
spent many hours trying novel ways to ignore pain. I was sure a few
times that the nurses were ignoring me on purpose, a nurses' revenge
on a doctor for making their life miserable. This is probably justifiable
punishment but quite paranoid on my part. Nighttime creates
outlandish thinking in insomniacs and I was not immune. Hours passed
monitored by which area was now aching more. I would try to will
the nurse to come. Maybe I could master telepathy – I never could.
No one saw I was in pain because I was unable to create any

expression on my face. Pain was a consistent partner for those first few weeks. I was unable to explain to anyone that I was in constant pain most of the time. An analgesic would have been appreciated, but then the problem would have been how to monitor my recovery. In any brain injury, the amount of alertness is a very important assessment.

My heart broke if I waited hours for someone to come and they didn't look at my face or didn't understand my blinking. It was my first lesson in frustration – first of many more to come. The faces of the nurses were my link to socialization. Instead of talking, I looked and listened to their stories. I delighted in those who chose to tell me about their lives: What their children were doing, what their husbands did on the weekend, their cars that needed repairs. Any topic, I didn't care, it was an escape from thinking. For that is all you can do while 'locked in' – think.

Faces, smiles, they meant so much. I will never forget my nurses, their faces, during those first few days. There was one nurse with the kindest smile whom I felt especially close to. She had long brown hair often tied back. She was about my age, mid-forties, and had a penchant to wear bobby socks over her white nylons. I felt like she cared, that this was more than just a job. She amused me and liked to sing while she worked around me. Her cheery attitude was what I needed.

I have an allergy problem that created a constant, congested nose. I usually use an allergy nasal spray at night; the information of such was not forwarded on to the nurses. For this reason, my nose was congested causing me aggravating discomfort. My inability to blow my nose would be an irritation for over a year. She recognized that this must be causing me problems, and she used suction to clear my nasal passages. Kind of embarrassing but such relief! Her care for me was so gentle and giving; she is always in my memory. I think her name was Nancy.

* * *

Music played for the first few days in my head. It was loud and classical. At first I thought the fellow in the bed beside me had his music awful loud. I searched the faces of the nurses working on me for a hint of their reaction to it. How could they let music play so loudly in an intensive care area? It was getting too much! *It is the middle of the night and they still allow him to play the radio! I can't sleep! Doesn't anyone care!*

It became apparent to me sometime that night that no one but I heard the music. It faded if someone spoke, but for the most part it was always present. I'm not sure when I became aware of these melodies because the first night is hazy in my memory, but for sure it was the first day after my stroke. The music was intricate but repetitive. When one song would finish, it was repeated. So much so, that I got annoyed. I was afraid I wouldn't get rid of this phenomenon. Thankfully, after awhile the melody would change.

I heard orchestration, with a predominance of violins. I marveled at how my brain could come up with such complex compositions. I imagined this was a side effect of the stroke. My patients neglected to mention this aspect of their strokes. I didn't remember reading about it. I supposed that a minor clot had hit the music center of my brain – wherever that is located – and excited it. It stopped after a few days.

It was a few months later that I started to wonder about the music. Why was it classical? If the music center of my brain had been triggered, it should have been rock, folk, or guitar music that was generated, not classical. I never listened to classical. It was not that I hated classical, I just hadn't taken the time to explore it. I was interested and I had meant to, but I never had listened to it, to the extent that I could come up with such complex rhythms, whether it was by memory or made up. Can our brains 'compose' this music on their own? Is it a phenomenon of a brain suddenly having no stimuli? Are we all potentially Mozarts?

Could it have been heavenly music?

I have not told many people about this phenomenon because of their reaction. Most people act very uncomfortable when I mention the music. I suppose they feel uncomfortable because they have nothing to say or don't know what to say. This is a normal reaction when engaged by someone with a subject we know nothing about, or have no opinion on that matter. We start moving about, stroking our hair, picking our fingers, or other such mannerisms, that indicate we are uncomfortable. Still others probably feel ol' Shawnie has lost it! The brainstem injury has rearranged a few neurons! Now he is going 'new age' on us! He will be wearing love beads next!

I really don't know what I heard. Does it have a scientific explanation or was it spiritual? I know I will be more attentive to the classics. I have always been spiritual and this has only reinforced my beliefs. Was it heavenly music I heard? I wonder.

*   *   *

So there was music, pain, and tubes. There were more tubes sticking out of my body. It may have been me supplying the music, if only I knew how to play them! There was the Foley from my penis, an endotracheal tube, an arterial line, an intravenous line (maybe a couple of those), and finally, a tube connected to pressure stockings on my legs.

I entertained myself by counting the respirator sounds. There was the shhhz-pop sound of the respirator, hour after hour, forcing itself into my unconscious thought. When I thought I had breathed in enough air, in would come a little bit more. I never thought I was in danger or that my survival depended upon the respirator. But it probably did.

The brainstem is also the site of the respiratory center. It tells the body when to inspire and expire. It is an involuntary action, an action we don't have to think about for it to happen. We can override this act (and hold our breath) by using our thoughts. As soon as we lose consciousness and faint, our brainstem takes over and we start to breath. No one knew if my respiratory center was damaged or not, but they couldn't take the chance. They slowly withdrew my ventilation support until I breathed on my own in a few days. I was eager to have it removed; I felt that I could breath just fine. In the spirit of how I thought – I was all right. The respiratory therapist would come in and tell me: I am doing fine. I thought they were being far too cautious but of course they weren't. The respirator needed to be withdrawn slowly.

I counted the inspiratory phase and compared it with my last count. Other people have reported to me they felt like they were in a constant state of panic while on the respirator. I did not feel like this. The respirator sound was kind of comforting, like having a grandfather's clock ticking in the hall. My inability to breathe on my own did not cause a feeling of suffocation. I just relaxed and went with it. I tried not to fight it, nor did I feel any need to do so.

When I tired of that count, there were my pressure stockings. They were pneumatic and automatic. They inflated with air from some pneumatic device on the floor and then deflated by some valve release, when a certain pressure was obtained. This keeps the blood flowing through the veins in my legs to prevent clots. This in turn prevents a condition called deep vein thrombophebitis, which if untreated can cause a life-threatening condition, when blood clots break off and rush to the lungs – a pulmonary embolism.

I counted to thirty-five on, thirty-five off. I saw how close my count was each time; wondering if it was really thirty seconds or if my counting was off. Amusing little games! The counting drove me crazy. Probably these little games were a defensive mechanism, an escape from my thoughts.

Living, thinking inside a dead body, what does one do? It would be a great premise for a Stephen King novel, for it was a living hell. What can you do? But think! That is all I could do and I did it constantly. I thought about my present circumstance, life, afterlife, family, and past. I did not dwell too much on the future at first because, as I have said, I was in denial. I'd be well in a few months. However I couldn't stop the negative thoughts from entering my mind. *What if I stayed like this!*

I decided soon that I couldn't live day after day deep in my thoughts. I needed an escape. This would ordinarily be reading, playing my guitar, or even work. I decided I needed a make-believe life, a place I could spend time in, maybe lead another life. Was it possible? I would later read Msr. Bambry's account of his life as a 'locked in' patient after he had a brainstem stroke in *The Diving Bell and the Butterfly.* He was able to let his imagination drift to other places. He imagined other places in the world he had visited in his life or read about, and he spent whole days wandering the streets of those imagination-fabricated towns. When he got tube feedings, he imagined being at fine restaurants dining on gourmet meals. He could actually taste the fine soups, followed by lamb, lobster, or whatever. I admire his ability to transcend the present and to exist in another world of his creation. I was not so strong.

I thought: *I will create a world of little creatures that live under trees, go on adventures. Ah…didn't Tolkien already do this? No matter, no one else knows. No copyrights in this world!* I set the scene, the characters (of course I would be the hero) and…. Pssst, some nurse described the cheesecake she had for lunch and I listened in. No matter, back I went into my dream world…. Pssst, "My daughter wants these designer jeans that cost seventy-five dollars when she could buy a perfectly good pair, the same thing without a fancy label, for thirty!", a nurse exclaimed from out of nowhere.

It was impossible! I was more interested in their lives than this Tolkienesque world which I created. I listened to their conversations, wishing I could join in with my views on designer clothes. Not that I had much to add, mind you! Thus ended my life as a mole in my dream world.

I regretted ignoring Jill in the past, telling me about her day while I had my nose stuck in the paper. How I wished I was there now. My heart leapt for joy whenever she came to see me in the ICU. I delighted in her telling me about the kids – what the doctor said – which friend sent supper over – what the day was like. Her presence was all I had to look forward to.

It was strange to have my children see me defenseless, vulnerable. Not that I ever tried to present myself as invincible, but I was the 'Dad'. They told me about school, what they were reading or doing, things a Dad wants to hear. My brother, Duane, was constantly at my side. My stepfather, Ron, and Mom were frequent visitors, and they were good companions for Jill in those first few weeks.

My mother gave me my first laugh. A priest, who was more of a friend, came to visit me. He was dressed in his priestly attire, as he had probably just visited a sick parishioner in hospital. My mother, Doreen, who was quite anxious and distraught over my condition, saw the priest at my bedside and jumped to conclusions. She took him aside – which she thought was out of my hearing range – and said, "Father, you aren't giving him the last rites are you?" If I had been capable of sound, they would have heard a loud guffaw.

I oriented myself in the NICU by imagining I was in a long corridor. Yet I knew this couldn't be true. I had visited the NICU many times in the past to visit patients. I knew it to be square with patients arranged along a wall, opposite the nursing desk, and along a wall to the left. It was spacious and kept dimly lit. The windows, which didn't open, were narrow and faced south. (The NICU is located on the fourth floor of the hospital. The Saint John Regional Hospital is located on a hill, outside of the central business section, in a forested area.) I was aware there were patients to either side of me, but I could not shake the notion: I was in a narrow room with patients aligned down one side.

Adding to my disorientation was the inability to move my neck; I looked in the direction they placed me. When they cautiously raised my head (they were afraid of creating dizziness), I could make out the nursing desk. The inability to look around frustrated me! I had double vision. The muscles of the eyeball cause this by not working synchronously. The nerves that control these muscles arise from the brain stem, in places called nuclei. My glasses compounded my problems with orientation. They were progressive bifocals; the bottom half is for reading. I could only look out of the bottom half while on my back, so everything was blurred. The view of the ceiling was great, though I believe I saw double the amount of dots in the ceiling tile.

I later met Eric, a fellow in my community who sustained a brainstem infarction a year before me. His double vision or diploplia never improved. He wears an eye patch to stop the diploplia, giving him monocular vision.

I started to suffer from headaches, I suppose brought on by these vision problems. They did not last too long into my convalescence but they were another problem I didn't need. I felt like a futuristic portrait of mankind – all brain and no body. But I did know I had a body – How it was misbehaving!

Depression crept in. Darkness, black, loneliness – the frustration of being unable to just get up, of being forced to lie there against my own will – my own body holding me captive. I wanted to go home with Jill, read my paper in my favourite chair, watch a movie with my children, anything but lie there. My worst time was the first Sunday after my stroke. They decided to get me up for the first time, in a pink chair that mechanically moved under me so they didn't have to lift me up. My first time out of bed. Instead of being joyous, I was filled with sadness.

They carefully brought the chair up from horizontal to a very small inclination in an upright position. I looked outside onto a clear blue sky. I was above the trees, which gently blew in the wind, and down the hill was the Red Cross building. The parking lot was pretty much vacant, reminding me that most people were home on this late Sunday afternoon. I would have been at the cottage, getting ready to depart for my home in town. I would have felt refreshed and recharged, anticipating a new week. Instead I lay there, wishing I could feel that breeze that I could see. It made me feel so blue. I missed Jill and my children. A feeling of unreality pervaded my soul. *This can't be happening!*

I never cried during those first few weeks. I seemed to be emotionally comatose. It was as though this sudden change in my function, from being a healthy caregiver to an invalid, was too much for my brain to comprehend. A nurse mistakenly thought I was crying when my eyes were tearing from some irritation. "Are you thinking too much?" she asked me, as she tenderly wiped the tears from my face.

I'm not crying! My eyes are burning out of my head! I tried to scream.

"Don't think. Try to rest. Let each day go by and who knows?"

I know. My eyes are about to expode!

Throughout this whole ordeal my face was expressionless. No one could read if I was in pain. The nurse was caring and I accepted her sympathy. I welcomed it but I welcomed more the cool towel she eventually got for me.

No one could read my face. My brother-in-law, Ted, bestowed on me a most beautiful discourse about my virtues and what I meant to him. All the while I was dying with a headache.

It was also strange to have my friends, fellow doctors, suddenly become my caregivers. Dr. Greg MacLean, a neurologist whom I knew as a comic actually acted like a neurologist. Dr. Sandy MacDougall whom I graduated with was looking after *me*. Dr. Peter Bailey whom I had less social contact with was my attending neurologist. Their visits to me, while I was in NICU, had an immediate effect upon my mood. I felt uplifted. I wondered if I had had that effect on my patients. Had I spent enough time by their bedside?

*   *   *

A week went by, and I survived on IV fluid, but this could not continue; I would need food. Since I was unable to swallow, a feeding tube had to be inserted. The best type for long-term use is a gastrotomy tube that is inserted into the stomach through the abdominal wall. The end inside the stomach has an inflatable bulb that prevents it from slipping out. Liquid supplements are given through the open end, enough to sustain one indefinitely.

The time had come for my endotracheal tube to be removed, as well. These tubes cannot remain in the trachea indefinitely. They stick out of the mouth and go into the windpipe or trachea. If one remains there, ulcers will form, infection and ultimately the breakdown of the air passages, a life-threatening situation. I was off the respirator and breathing on my own. Yet I was not ready to breathe on my own because my epiglottis (the valve on the top of the trachea that prevents fluid or food from entering the lungs) was not working. I would be aspirating saliva, tube feed I burped up, and gastric juices. My lungs had to be protected. Besides, my muscles of respiration were not strong enough to pull the air into my lungs. It requires much less energy to breathe through a hole in your throat.

A tracheostomy is performed inserting a tube below the larynx or voice box into the trachea. This tracheostomy tube or trach for short has an inflatable bulb on one end that prevents debris from entering the lungs. It completely seals off the lungs from the outside. I headed to the OR for the insertion of both of these tubes about one week after I had entered the ICU.

Everything went well except I had a big problem: without the tube, I bit down on my tongue. The muscles of mastication or chewing were set to 'on'. The inhibitory signal, to relax, was not getting through. My jaws were clenched tight and unfortunately my tongue was between my teeth.

The nurses tried putting an oral airway in. This is a plastic device that goes from your mouth to the back of your throat. No manner of twisting, prodding, or force got that oral airway between my teeth. Besides, they were hurting my tongue. Then they decided to try tongue depressors. They succeeded in wedging in some depressors after many attempts and at a cost to my tongue. I dreaded the moment I saw them come with more tongue depressors. "I think we'll give it another try, Shawn."

Leave me alone! My tongue is fine! I tried to cry.

I was wrong. Jill later told me they had to do something; my tongue had turned blue and yellow. It was grossly swollen from me biting it. Why I did not feel this? I have no idea.

The tongue depressor idea did not last; they wouldn't stay in place. We needed a more permanent solution. Someone came up with the idea of dental clamps used to keep your mouth open during dental surgery. Who to better put them in but my dentist. It was a surprise to open my eyes one evening and see Dr. Shane Holt, my dentist, in front of me! He decided to give me a muscle relaxant through the IV and then put the clamp in. It worked and I looked a sight!

I remained with that dental clamp sticking out of my mouth for days. They switched it to the other side of my mouth, days later, to prevent mouth ulcers, which meant another dentist had to visit – Dr. Murray Holburn. A week later I yawned and the clamp fell out. I would spend months trying to open my mouth further.

One day Doug Gainsforth, my speech pathologist, came in with what he called an eye gaze board. Prior to this, he had been trying to stimulate my swallowing by using metal instruments that he immersed in ice, then applied to the back of my throat. I could reflexively swallow but not initiate a swallow. Jill was encouraged each time I swallowed, but I could tell by his reaction that he was not impressed. That type of swallow did not mean a functional swallow; it was a reflex. Indeed, his cold stimulation did not produce a voluntary swallow.

Suspicious of this eye gaze board, I listened to his explanation of how to use it. I thought: *I will be a good patient and humour him. I will learn how to use it but I won't need it long. I will be talking soon – as soon as they remove this trach – which won't be long – I'll be singing.* It was easy enough to understand how to use it, and before long I had my first conversation. Significantly, one of the first things I asked him was, "When will I be able to talk?"

His answer was evasive. I expected him to say, "Maybe a couple of weeks, Shawn." Instead it was, "awhile." *What did that mean! Of course he couldn't say anything; he wasn't my doctor. Why was everybody being so careful!* I was used to the health world. No one likes to take responsibility because they may say the wrong thing. This is what I thought was happening. To some extent, that was true, but in reality they were sparing my feelings. It was probably a good approach. I don't think I could have handled reality at that point. Denial can be O.K.; a defensive mechanism we use when the truth is too hard to accept.

Jill took to the eye board eagerly. It was great to be able to finally converse with her. It wasn't easy though. It was hard for the person trying to follow my eyes. My eyes, as I have said, were not acting together. I was often mixed up, as I saw double, especially in certain directions, and which eye were they to follow! Letter by letter, Jill and I would plod along. The conversations had to be kept superficial, as it was tiresome for my eyes and they would soon tear.

My parents found it difficult and as my mother would later tell me, her heart was never really into it because she, like me, thought I would be talking before too long. The eye gaze board wasn't a useful tool in interacting with the nurses – most weren't familiar with it.

Now that I was off the respirator, I was ready to leave the

NICU. My first big step in recovery! I had stayed in the unit for 12 days. Nights, days, they all ran together. I felt like screaming, *"Now we're getting somewhere!"*

CHAPTER 4 – THE FLOOR

I was introduced to my new room: a ward of four beds – two beds along opposite walls with a bathroom between 2 windows. The wall to the corridor was all glass and located beside the nursing desk so that the patients could be observed.

I was placed next to one of the windows, much to my delight. All I could see was the sky but it gave me a sense of freedom. I felt a sense of accomplishment by being released from ICU. I had achieved a step towards recovery, but at this point my idea of recovery was total and I had no idea the ladder out was so long.

I was excited about moving onto the floor. It had been twelve days of observing the ceiling, listening to fragments of conversations, watching the nurses as they came into my field of vision, and listening to my thoughts –thinking, thinking, thinking. Television would be a welcome diversion.

A major disappointment – I could not get comfortable to watch TV. When someone did manage to get me into a comfortable position, my diploplia or double vision thwarted any obtained pleasure. I was uninterested in TV, anyway. I looked upon news and sports with indifference – which I had always enjoyed. Were my physical disabilities frustrating me and preventing me from enjoying TV, or was it my mental state?

Lack of concentration, insomnia, and the inability to enjoy simple pleasures are symptoms of depression. I had reason to be depressed, but I didn't *feel* depressed.

I think it was healthy that I began to notice the other patients and their families. I later became friends with a man who lay in the bed beside me in the NICU. Kevin and I were oblivious to one another a few feet apart but met hundreds of miles away at Stan Cassidy Centre for Rehabilitation.

On the floor, I became aware of my surroundings. The man beside me was confused and kept trying to get out of bed. His family was attentive and stayed by his side. I thought I smiled, when they looked over, inviting a comment but my face was not expressing my intent. Little wonder I received no response. I must have looked like I was brain dead, a vegetable, alive, but not really aware. I didn't think of how people perceived me. I didn't care. I had more important matters to contend with.

Pain was still ever present. The nurses could spend less time with me on the floor and I had a whole new group to educate what my furious blinking meant. Most of them knew to look at me, but occasionally one didn't look at me – they did their job and left. That was disappointing if I had been waiting to tell someone about a pain, but it didn't matter much. Moving a limb was usually all that was necessary to resolve the pain, however within a matter of minutes, a pain would be back in the same leg, at a different spot – futile. I'm not sure why I didn't request more analgesia (pain killers).

Sleep was difficult. It was very frustrating. I longed for a break from the constant thinking; my mind exploring every possibility; a break from the aching in my legs; a break from my blurred vision; so weary, so weary.

The reticular activating system, an area responsible for the act of falling asleep, is located in the brainstem. It can be affected by a brainstem stroke. In my case, it definitely was altered. I spent countless hours looking at the drapes. I would cat nap throughout the night. They tried me on mild sedatives that had no effect. Weeks went by with little sleep.

It was not worth the effort to tell a nurse at three am, I am not sleeping. What could they do? Better to try again with another medication, tomorrow night. I watched the sitter read, played mind games, and battled with my thoughts.

They hired sitters to watch over me during the night. I wasn't able to ring a bell for help and they were still uncomfortable about my breathing. It wasn't very practical: it was hard for the sitters to observe me in the dark, batting my eyelashes for help. A few times they did see me, but most of the time – I gave up.

It was strange to be near the sitters, night after night, and never talk. I would experience this feeling many times in the months to come. I enjoyed talking to people; this is what I did every day, and I had grown from a shy young man to a confident person in relating to people. I wanted to ask them about university, their families, sports, anything. Instead, I watched them and thought.

I thought of Jill, my children, my parents, and my patients. I have learned so much over 20 years from my medical practice. So many lives; so many stories; so much pain; so much love; I had many memories to keep me entertained.

* * *

I took over an existing family practice from a well-liked doctor by the name of Dr. Norbert Grant. He had started his practice of medicine after serving in the war. Over the years, he had developed quite a following of patients, who were all very fond of him. When he retired, he asked me to take over his practice. Fresh out of medical school I came to take over this group who were sorry to see Dr. Grant go, anticipating me changing things, screwing up their medications, never being available, and God knows what else!

I did initiate many changes, but so did I change. His patients and I, for the most part, gradually grew to accept each other and thus began 20 years of wonderful relationships. I was warned in medical school that a doctor couldn't afford to get too involved in the lives or feelings of patients. The transference of feelings can weigh too heavy on caregivers; to remain strong, you have to divorce yourself from their feelings. Caregivers will do them no good if they get sick too. I had a hard time preventing a strong emotional bond from forming with some patients.

Kathleen was in her nineties; she was thin, grey-haired, frail, but mentally very sharp. She lived with her daughter, who was in her seventies, in an apartment complex designed for those of low income. I made home visits to her; her health was too poor for her to come to my office and over time I began to look forward to my visits. She enthralled me with tales of her life, her husband, and the city in earlier years. She never complained much but I could see her breathing was becoming more laboured with time. She was dying of heart failure and all the drugs in the world were not going to help this tired, old heart.

She made me laugh. I was comfortable in her presence and I fell in love with her. She had me wrapped around her finger.

One day, while I was working in my office, I got a call from Kathleen. She said she was short of breath and asked if I could come to see her? I told her of course I would, but it would be a few hours. I had an office full of patients and I was booked for the whole day. All seemed well at that point and the day was going by quickly when I received another call from Kathleen.

I could tell from her voice that things were not right. She had called me back to tell me her breathing was worse. I could hear the unmistakable sound of someone in pulmonary edema. (That is a condition of fluid backing up in the lungs from a failing heart.) I told her I was calling an ambulance, right now, to take her to hospital. She begged me not to do that, she was all right; she would wait for me.

I reluctantly agreed to her request but I felt uneasy. As I finished the patients remaining in my waiting room, I kept thinking that I should have been more forceful with her. I shouldn't have let Kathleen talk me into letting her stay. I finally left my office in haste, after the last patient. As I approached her apartment building, I saw her daughter watching out for me from the front window.

I heard Kathleen before I saw her. Her breathing was laboured and her colour ashen. I knew before I placed my stethoscope on her back that I would hear rales or bubble sounds, up most of her lungs. She was in massive pulmonary edema. Her heart was not in an abnormal rhythm to explain her failure; rather it was in a regular, slow beat. The pump or heart was failing. If she were to get through this, she would need IV furosemide – a drug used to flush fluid out of the body.

"Do I have to go? I hate the hospital," she asked between breaths.

"I need to give you a drug to make you pee out fluid. I have to give it to you. You should have gone to hospital when I said," I chastised her.

"If you say so, Doc."

"I know so. It's the only way to get you comfortable."

I waited with her until the ambulance came and then followed them to the hospital. I wrote my orders, admission, history, and all seemed well. The diuretic had started to work by the time I left. I joked with her about something silly and left feeling that it was a job well done.

I was late getting home that evening. We were still living in an apartment on the east side of Saint John. I had been home only about half an hour when the doctor who was working Emergency called:

"I know you're not on call, but I think you would want to know; your patient you admitted tonight, Kathleen . . . has just passed away."

"Wha-at!"

"Yeah, she was doing fine and the nurses were just about to take her up to the floor when she stopped breathing. Appears that her heart just stopped. You had a no code order, so I just pronounced her."

"Is her daughter still there?" I asked.

"Yeah, she was right beside her when she took her last breath. Talking right up until the end, apparently."

"Can I talk to her?"

I said the usual – 'I'm sorry', 'tried my best', 'guess her heart was too old', 'going to miss her'. After I hung up, I started to cry. Bewildered, I went into my bedroom, lay down, and sobbed.

I cried over losing her; I cried because I thought I would save her; I was frustrated, tired from the day, probably from many reasons. Jill consoled me, though she probably thought it was a strange reaction – I had had patients die before. But I had broken the rule with her and had become too close. I would never again cry over losing a patient. I learned my lesson; there needs to be a wall between the doctor and the patient. I always felt close to my patients but I never forgot: they were patients. It worked as a protection for me, to prevent emotional strain, as well as a positive for my patients. Doctors don't make good clinical judgments when too close to the situation. This would be a struggle – it is hard not to become immersed in a patient's joy or sorrow after knowing them for twenty years.

* * *

My tube feedings had started in the NICU by syringing an amount of supplement directly into my stomach tube. The amount they used had no effect on me; it made me neither full nor hungry. However, it resulted in a certain form of nursing duty to spring into action; they decided I needed a bowel movement. I don't know what type of suppository they used but it caused excruciating cramps. It could have been that I didn't need to go. It could have been that I was constipated. It could have been the wrong type of suppository. I don't know what was the matter but it was my first taste of being a *real* patient.

As the suppository worked, they placed a sheet under my bum and I was to defecate on this. A novel experience! I never imagined I could do such a thing but it wasn't hard; you had no choice! The little suppository worked its magic and presto! I never got used to having a bowel movement in bed but I had no choice; I couldn't sit up and it would be months before I could. At least they found a type of suppository that didn't cause so much cramping,

Another nursing duty they carried out with military precision was turning me. I was to be turned every two hours to prevent bedsores and also for comfort. This probably didn't help my sleep but I welcomed it; it relieved my aches and pains, if only temporarily.

By this time, my catheter had been removed from my bladder – not an altogether painful procedure, I am glad to report – and I had a condom catheter in place.

In the ICU, the occupational therapist had fashioned splints for my arms and legs. The arms and hands tend to go into a flexed, contracted position and the legs and feet tend to become extended. The splints are used to try to prevent this. It was uncomfortable and hot having both arms and legs splinted for two hours. They would remove them for two hours and then repeat this schedule, day and night. I knew they were necessary but that didn't make the wearing of them easier.

Physiotherapists started stretching exercises. My knees would be flexed high onto my chest, my arms high over my head. There, I thought, *certainly they can see I am supple and my recovery will be quick. I bet they're amazed at how good I am!*

I denied the truth, or at least I wasn't thinking; in any spinal injury there is a period of 'spinal shock' in which the muscles are flaccid before they become rigid. I wanted to continue to believe I was going to recover quicker than they anticipated. I thought I would astound them; instead, I astounded myself.

Dr. Bailey asked if I would be willing to go to Stan Cassidy, the tertiary centre for rehabilitation in the province. It is located in Fredericton, the capital city of New Brunswick, a little over an hour's ride from Saint John. I agreed: the transfer would happen soon.

Before this transfer occurred, I had a MRI (Magnetic Resonance Image). The head nurse, Janice Kenny, or Loopdy, as I knew her, came with me. It was a strange sensation to be a 'real patient', on a stretcher, wheeling through familiar corridors, watching the lights and ceiling tile going by over my head, seeing staff I had interacted with a scant week ago – now I was the patient.

The MRI was small and noisy; the banging seemed out-of-place for such a precise, techno-machine. The MRI requires that you spend a fair amount of time inside; rhythms developed in my head, to the fans circulating the air. Loopdy stayed by my side watching my trach (tracheotomy tube) for congestion.

The MRI showed the infarction (area of cell death) to be on the pons – a part of the brainstem that looks like a walnut. It measured 21mm x 12mm – less than an inch long and about ½ inch deep. It is hard to conceive that such a small area can cause such devastation. A small linear area had died as well on my cerebellum – an appendage on the base of the brain, used mainly for balance, that looks like a slice of cauliflower.

I know the area of infarct was close to the respiratory centre, so I'm lucky to be alive. But my life has changed dramatically due to that 21 millimetre – a pathetically small injury for destroying a multitude of dreams. It didn't seem right.

That same day, Patti, my nurse friend who worked on the neurological floor, took my mother and Jill up to see Stan Cassidy Centre for Rehabilitation. They felt comfortable with the staff but they were surprised at how small and old the building was.

Meanwhile, I was having problems with my ears. I have had hearing problems since I was a little boy. It seemed to start from a deviated septum or a broken nose incurred while playing hockey. There was also an allergy problem, causing excessive mucous production, which in turn blocked the auditory tubes. All of the above resulted in repeated ear infections, with scarring of the tympanic membranes (eardrums) being the outcome.

I felt another earache develop. Besides the pain I became deaf as more fluid built up in my middle ear. I could not hear anyone speak. For a few days, I experienced what it must be like to be speech impaired and deaf. I worried about being unable to hear my therapist's instructions to enable me to improve.

The otolaryngologist, Dr. Tees, came to my rescue. He proposed to put tubes in my ears and he did the day before I left the Regional Hospital. I could hear things I hadn't heard in years. I should have done this years ago but I was always 'too busy'.

The process of going to the OR was easy. I felt no anxiety – after all, how could things get worse? – I simply fell asleep once the anaesthetist gave me his magic needle and woke up in recovery. Again I marvelled at my lack of concern. Normally I would have experienced cramps, sweaty palms, maybe some light-headedness before the surgery. But I was calm, unconcerned, and cool.

The next day I was ready to leave the Regional for Stan Cassidy. It had been two and a half weeks since my stroke and I was eager to go. Friends and nurses came to say good-bye. I lifted my left thumb in response to their encouragement; the first movement in my limbs that returned. I expected my right thumb would start moving shortly. Eighteen months later, I cannot do it.

It was a beautiful Monday morning when I left Saint John. I was to be transported up by ambulance, and for the first time I felt a twinge of anxiety. My trach congested periodically and required suctioning, a hideous but necessary procedure. Did this ambulance attendant know how to do this? Could I last until I got to my destination? With these questions, I left the hospital. I was sure I wouldn't be long at the rehab. I am glad I didn't know the truth.

CHAPTER 5 – STAN CASSIDY CENTRE FOR REHABILITATION

It was the hottest May 31 we ever had. Great! I spent it in the back of an ambulance, breathing through a tube in my neck, wrapped up in blankets with no air conditioning!

I was impressed by how clean it was in the back of the ambulance. I was able to see the sky out the back door window, so I amused myself by orienting our position on the highway by the turns and hills the ambulance took. *Now we're going along Harbour Bridge, should be stopping soon at the tollbooth.* I verified whether I was right or not by high landmarks that could be seen out the window.

The closer we got to Fredericton, the hotter it became. We soon found the air conditioning in the ambulance was not working.

Sweat entered my eye. The attendant tried to make me comfortable but how could I tell him my eyes were burning? It is amazing to me now how I endured the minor irritations. How often does your scalp itch, your mouth get a little too moist, or your nose itch? Little things a quick touch with your hand solves. A lot! You just accept the fact that you can't scratch that itch and eventually it goes.

It is not really that simple. There were plenty of times I had to endure an itch or a burn. I dreamed to get my mind off it. On this trip, with my eyes burning, my mind drifted again to my experiences…

* * *

The Emergency department was always an adventure. I worked Emergency for twelve years until it wasn't a requirement for GP's in our area. By this time, a new breed of doctor had emerged, the emergentologist, and as more of these doctors came into our community, I felt it was a good time to leave and concentrate on my family practice.

Emergency medicine can make you feel great one minute and terrible the next. A patient dies, and there is no time to recoup, for it's time to move to the next patient. The same holds true in the office but at a slower pace: informing a patient they have cancer and dealing with the emotional trauma that creates, and within a few minutes having to act cheerful with the next patient, who may be a child.

The adrenaline rush can be addictive: cardiac arrests, multiple trauma, etc. There was no greater feeling than success, and no greater low than failure. I feared that I might order the wrong thing, that I might forget something, that I might go blank, that I might cost his or her life. Thankfully that never happened.

The hustle and bustle of emergency work caused its own adrenaline rush without being confronted by life-threatening emergencies. In fact, I could not go home and fall asleep; I had to unwind first, no matter how tired I was.

Not all the work is urgent; about seventy-five percent are minor problems: colds, earaches, cuts, sprains, and other odd ailments.

A night to be remembered had to be when a busload of people overturned on the highway. I was terrified with the confusion and mayhem of suddenly being confronted with thirteen victims. I called in lots of help that night. The worst night, however, had to be the night a young, drunk driver collided with two women and their children on the way to a Halloween party. He came up an off-ramp the wrong way. He smashed into the car containing the two moms and their children. They had nowhere to turn; they had just come off the highway onto this off-ramp. I can imagine the horror they felt as they knew what was about to happen and had no way to avoid it.

The young man was the first one brought into the Emergency

Department. He was drunk and pretty badly broken up with multiple fractures, lacerations, and possible internal damage. He was conscious and yelling like a banshee.

We learned that the young mother who was driving had died at the scene, but the others were all right. The young girl, whose mother had died, was brought into the trauma room carried by her Dad, a policeman. Can you imagine being called to the scene of an accident and finding out it's your wife and daughter?

The scene of this policeman carrying in his little girl, knowing his wife had just died, appeared so tragic. The drunk driver chose that moment to cry out for his mother. He cried, "Mommy, Mommy!" in a loud, sobbing voice. I wouldn't have been surprised if the policeman had drawn his revolver and shot the guy. To his credit, he said nothing; quietly spoke to his daughter while the nurses took them to another area. I felt like harming a patient for the first and only time in my career. I felt like leaning on his broken leg or pulling his catheter or 'mistakenly' move his IV. The more he wailed, the more I wanted to hurt him. I didn't. Eventually we stabilized him and sent him to the OR. I never forgot that cold night, the policeman and his daughter, and my anger. This same scenario is played over and over, too many times, at too many places. Drinking and driving has to be dealt with harshly; it is intolerable.

*   *   *

My eyes stopped burning and before long we were at Stan Cassidy Centre for Rehabilitation. My mother and Jill were there to greet me. I was shocked at the appearance of the Centre. I expected the tertiary care centre of rehabilitative medicine for the province of New Brunswick to be a modern facility; instead it was a low, white, cement and obviously old building. It definitely had a 50's feel to it, and in fact just outside the front door was a stone with the date on it, 1957.

Two people from Saint John greeted me at the front door as I wheeled through: Dwight Allaby and Barbie Clark. Barbie was an old friend – the improbability that two old friends should end up here, at the same time, far from home, in a rehabilitation centre, struck me.

Barbie had suffered spinal cord trauma from a motor vehicle accident. At this point, no one knew how much function would return. She was extremely lucky to escape with her life; and even luckier still, most function will return to her legs. We grew up in a small summertime community called Sand Point. I had just visited her on the neurological floor of the Saint John Regional Hospital about a week before my stroke.

Dwight had a complete paralysis from the neck down as a rare complication of a viral infection. It would take over a year, but eventually he would have good use of his hands and be able to walk with a cane.

They greeted me outside the entrance to the cafeteria. The walls inside were made of the same cement blocks as outside, giving the whole area a cold feel. They tried in the cafeteria to liven it up with different colours, but it didn't hide the fact: they were cement blocks.

I was whisked down a corridor, a quick stop at the nurses' desk, and then on to my room, number 8. The walls were the same cement blocks, painted white. The outer wall had many windows looking out onto a courtyard. The courtyard was enclosed on three sides by the building and featured a gazebo in the centre. Along the walls of the building were planted perennials and shrubs. They were sadly not maintained and weeds were allowed to grow amongst them, adding to the neglected feel to the rehab. The sad little flowers reflected the financial strain that rehabilitative medicine was under in this province.

My room had a sink, and in a little room off to the side there was a toilet – which I would never use. A closet was located along the same wall as the toilet room and sink.

I was shocked at these conditions. I had worked all my life in a modern hospital setting. I tried not to show it; I tried to make the best of it, but I was disappointed.

That feeling did not last long because in came the head nurse. Any dour feelings evaporated as soon as she came into the room. Louise was a pretty girl, with long blonde hair, a sunny personality, and the manner of complete confidence. She was British, with a thick accent, most unusual for this bilingual institution. I was astounded that this young woman could be the head nurse, but I was soon shown why, as she took charge.

Over the coming months I grew to appreciate Louise, and my fellow patients and I were confident in her judgments. She was amazingly strong for her build. She was single and owned a farm. She enthralled me with stories of her goat, Peaches. Peaches, it seems, was quite possessive of her and had a nasty habit of butting gentlemen callers. Perhaps that is why she was still single.

After introductions and the arranging of my room, she began to wash me because of my sweaty journey. My face, then chest, over onto one side to do my back, and then she said, in her British accent, "Now it's time to do your nooks and crannies!"

My mind quickly reeled through all the anatomy I knew. *Must be an English thing. Behind the ears? No. The armpits? No. The toes! That's it! No. Oh no! It can't be!!!*

To my horror and before I could think little else, my diapers were off and there I was, exposed and vulnerable. Without a word, soap and water were slapped on and I was dried and diapered before I had time for embarrassment.

It soon became routine; there is no place for modesty in the disabled world. I had to get used to the idea of having strangers invade my private person. The bed baths, the genitalia washed twice a day, the bowel routine, having my bum wiped, putting on a condom catheter – all necessary, but so hard to endure. The act of having someone else wipe your bum was the hardest to endure. I knew the nurses were professionals and this was part of their job, so I never felt I lost my dignity.

After my introduction to Stan Cassidy and Louise, the nurses took off my regulation hospital wear and dressed me in street clothes. I was surprised but already I felt positive about this: It was my first step in rehabilitation.

I had my first visit from an Occupational Therapist (OT) who brought with her a wheelchair. I lay in, rather than sat in, my chair, which had a headrest for my wobbly head. I could not hold up my head at this point but it became one of the first things I could do. They were afraid I might become dizzy and nauseated on getting up and moving, but I didn't. It felt good to be finally mobile. Mom and Jill took me outside that afternoon.

I couldn't turn my head or see much, but the air felt good. I closed my eyes and breathed in, finally free of those institutional smells. I savoured the experiences of sun on my skin, the sound of wind moving through trees, cars going by, and people talking – normal sounds and smells and sensations. The people around me talked about common things, things that weren't about me. A world other than sickness; it felt so good!

Time outside quickly ended, and soon I was back in bed. At the Regional, I was accustomed to continuous humidity for my trach. Here I was introduced to intermittent humidity. Humidity is moisture that is given through the air breathed in to keep the lungs moist. At Stan Cassidy they used some archaic device from years back that surprised me. A nebulizer (like a small plastic cup) was hooked into a hollow tube that ran from my trach to a small air compressor. It was the air compressor that surprised me. It was noisy and looked old. The nebulizer was tricky; it had to be held a certain way or it wouldn't work and since I had no hand control, it often took longer than necessary to finish.

If you wanted air at the Regional, you just plugged into the wall and adjusted the flow. I had trained and worked at modern hospitals all my life; Stan Cassidy was looking poor to me so far. They were supposed to help me?

If I thought the aerosol machines were old, I had a greater shock at the condition of the suction machines. At the Regional, the suction outlets were on the wall and you adjusted the degree of suctioning wanted. At Stan Cassidy, they brought in an old suction device that I hadn't seen in years. This baby was ancient and noisy.

They decided to use continuous feeds rather than bolus feeding via my gastrotomy. They do this with a machine that regulates the rate at which the liquid flows in. Finally, a device I was quite familiar with and state of the art.

I had expected so much more from Stan Cassidy than what I was seeing. I ended my first day with a heavy heart. But this blue feeling was counteracted by news that Jill was staying with me for the first night. They arranged for Jill to sleep in a bed beside me for this one night. It was exciting, like having a camp-over when we were kids. It would have been so nice to talk with Jill, eat popcorn, watch a movie, maybe hold hands, but it could not happen. I was content enough to have her in the same room.

They didn't trust my breathing; they were afraid it might suddenly stop. Dr. Bailey arranged for an apneic device to be attached to my chest, I bet more to reassure Jill than because of the probability. This would ring an alarm if I stopped breathing. After a few nights of alarms ringing for no reason, I asked them to give it up. Sleep was more important than breathing by this point!

So ended my first day at Rehab; I was filled with mixed feelings, happy to have Jill at my side, happy to be on the road to recovery, but disappointed in Stan Cassidy. I was soon to learn that Stan Cassidy was more than met the eye. The next day I met my physiotherapist, occupational therapist, and speech pathologist. They became my whole life. For the next ten months, they were my daily routine. They were my world. They were my hope.

CHAPTER 6 – JUNE

I was still in denial in the early part of June, and the whole experience seemed unreal to me. I was more willing to concede that I would have to take the summer off. I didn't want to be here, but I was willing to stay for faster improvement. I fully expected to return to work by the fall.

Jill or my mother often stayed at Kiwanis House nearby – low cost accommodations for families of patients, provided by Stan Cassidy Centre. It's located just behind the Centre. Jill and my mother vowed I would not be left alone, due to my helplessness.

Jill or Mom would often wheel me out to the courtyard under the gazebo and read to me. I was often hot because of the white anti-embolic stockings and diapers; my eyes burned when exposed to the sun or air; and my surrounding environment was blurry, due to my vision. But despite all of the above, it felt good to be outside. A pleasant hour could be spent there with Jill or Mom reading to me and I could lose myself for a short time; welcome relief from the reality of being 'locked in'.

There is a park beside the Centre featuring huge weeping willows. A gravel pathway meanders through the small park. There are areas for barbeques, another gazebo, and two small bridges over a marsh. I loved to sit under a willow, feeling the branches touch my face, and gaze upon the marsh. I knew there had to be frogs in the marsh and I thought I would sit and wait until I saw one. A dragonfly might light on one of those cattails. I wished a bird would fly into my little scene. I felt as though I could be happy here. *Perhaps,* I thought, *I could plant some flowers out here and tend to them every day.*

The park was also the victim of under financing. The gazebo was in need of repair, the fire pit had not seen the warmth of fire for a long time, and weeds were growing in containers that should have been alive with flowers. Patients seldom used the park; most of us were too beaten up in body or spirit to enjoy it, but it was a welcome reprieve from the Centre when we did visit.

Reality struck and my behind cried out for relief from this wheelchair seat, or my trach became congested, signalling time to head back for suctioning. What was I thinking? I couldn't stay away for any length of time before I needed nursing assistance. I guess I saw potential in this park as a place to get away from the daily nursing routine, a little area to fulfill my need for independence and solitude. It never happened.

My visits were cut short because of my need for suctioning. Suctioning! Anyone who has ever had a tracheotomy tube can relate the delights of suctioning the tube. It is required because more phlegm is produced in the lungs with the trach present. Combined with my weak expirations, the phlegm had to be manually removed.

A sterile, thin, plastic tube is hooked up to a suction device and inserted down the trach into the windpipe. The suction, while removing phlegm, also takes out a lot of air from the lungs, and for a moment I felt as though I was suffocating. I tried desperately to breath in, but couldn't. The suctioning tube causes a reflex cough to occur but most of my air had been suctioned out, so, while I was frantic for air, at the same time I had to cough. Confused? There is a moment of panic while the suctioning tube is being withdrawn. This all occurs in a matter of seconds as the nurses suction quickly, but what a few seconds!

It's amazing what the human body learns to tolerate, because after a few months of this, I really don't mind the suctioning. In fact, having the phlegm rattle around in my trach tube is more bothersome than the procedure, and I end up begging the nurses or Jill to have it done.

* * *

The next day after my arrival I met my three therapists, who became so very important to me. Beth McCann is my Speech Pathologist. She is middle-aged with thin blonde hair that hangs down to her shoulders. She laughs easily and has a love of cats. I saw her twice a day, five days a week, as she helped me swallow again, then eat, make my first sounds, and then finally, start to articulate. Sometimes the tasks were tedious, sometimes the tasks were difficult; more than often they met with failure, but mainly due to her, I never gave up.

Doreen Legere is my Occupational Therapist. She is tall (they all look tall from a wheelchair) from the Miramichi area of New Brunswick, and with a constant smile (again smiles – that seems so important to me). She is the sort of person you instantly like. She is down-to earth and has a huge laugh. She concentrates on my hands, sit-to-stand, bed mobility, wheelchair, and how the environment can be adapted to suit my disability. She came to know when to push and when to back off. I was always amazed at the amount of energy she expended on my behalf. I value her friendship today.

Mereille (pronounced Me-ray) Ouellette is my physiotherapist. She is of average size and build, a French-Canadian, with a smile that is a constant source of reassurance to me. I gained strength from her enthusiasm for every small achievement. I grew dependent upon her: I watched her reaction for any small sign on her face that I'd been a good boy – that I did my exercises well.

Her eyes were expressive and her smile warmed my spirit. She was always optimistic about my recovery and I owe her the drive I still have to improve. Her greatest gift to me was hope.

These three girls became my world for the next ten months. Anything they said I tried to do. I left my shingle at the front door. I didn't feel much like a physician anyway, so it wasn't hard.

My weekdays were pretty full with my three therapists. The nurses awoke me at 6 A.M. to start my tube feedings, so it would be over before my therapies started. I was washed and ready for 8:30. I usually started with speech therapy for half an hour, then physiotherapy for an hour, physiotherapy and occupational therapy combined for a half hour, and then finally OT alone for a half hour. Then it was time for lunch, which in my case was another can or two of that delicious tube feed. After lunch I had another hour of physiotherapy, followed by another half hour of speech, and finally a half hour of OT. By this time it was 3 or 4 PM and I rested before "supper".

It sounds exhausting to me as I write about it now, but I was never that physically tired. Fatigue is very common after a stroke and I was lucky not to have experienced it too bad. I prayed every night for strength.

My days were busy, little time for introspection, but the weekends were another matter. The entire therapy staffs were gone for the weekend; no therapies took place. Patients were encouraged to go home as part of their rehabilitation. So it was only a few of us poor schmucks who remained. The joint was dead! I had Jill, family, and friends with me for which I'm forever grateful. Still there were times when I had nothing but time. My eyes tired from trying to 'talk' and my responses were short. My memories were my companion….

*   *   *

Art and Hilda – I inherited them from another physician who left town, and by this time Art had already suffered two strokes. He walked with a quad cane (it has a platform with 4 rubber ends for greater stability) while the affected arm was in a permanent flexed position. He spoke out of the side of his mouth.

Art loved to talk. I hardly got a word in during my home visits with him. He loved to watch the parliamentary channel on TV, even though it agitated him. He delighted in telling me what the politicians were doing wrong. The longer I let him speak, the more agitated he became, and the worse his blood pressure reading would be. I learned to take his blood pressure right away if the parliamentary channel was on. It would invariably be much better than if I waited until after his discourse on politics.

I loved the guy; he was humorous and he loved to tell me of 'the old days'. Hilda would chide Art, telling him he had said enough and that he had to let the doctor do his work. Sometimes it was hard to get everything done, but I didn't mind; I loved to hear him talk.

Hilda was always just as friendly. She was a thinly built woman who wore a permanent smile. She hung on Art's every word, admonishing him for repeating a story he told me last month. You could tell she worshiped him and they had had a life-long partnership of love. Their son and his family lived in the flat above them, so they had plenty of help if needed. I had a feeling Hilda didn't often ask for help.

As years went by, Art suffered repeated small strokes that left him more physically challenged, and sadly, more confused. The post-infarct dementia developed slowly. I could see his responses to my questions becoming more bizarre and finally there was no spoken interaction. It pained me to see this once friendly, talkative, proud man become this fellow who just stared at me.

Hilda continued to talk to him, comb his hair, and fix his shirt to look presentable. The love I had felt between the two had not changed. Art was unable to show Hilda the love he felt for her, but this had not changed anything; she knew her Art was still there. Hilda was not a big woman, but still she dressed him and helped him to his favourite chair. This must have taken a lot of effort and we had to face facts – maybe it was time to start thinking of nursing homes. She would laugh gently and tell me they were doing just fine. Why they were still going for drives!

Art had spent his life around cars and owned a car repair garage. He visibly got excited when he was going for a car ride. I couldn't imagine how she managed to get him – now unable to walk without a lot of support – into a car.

Where did they go? Hilda told me where they always went – up the river road to Grand Bay. There they would sit in the car and have an ice cream while watching the boats sailing on the bay. I pictured them in happier times, laughing, talking, being together. They were still in each other's company, but Hilda carried on the conversation or sometimes they sat in silence, just glad in being together.

One day Hilda showed up at my office looking rather pale, saying that she was tired. She looked ill and I quickly arranged for some blood tests to be done. When the tests came back they pointed to a form of leukemia. I arranged for her to be admitted to the hospital the next day. Meanwhile, Art's family upstairs would look after him.

In hospital, we found that Hilda had an especially aggressive form of leukemia. It didn't look good considering her age, but the haematologist offered her a chance with some chemotherapy. It would be rough; the chemo could make her sick and at her age (in the 80's) would she be able to take it? I probably should have advised her not to try, but this happened so fast I hadn't got used to the idea of Hilda being sick. I had to try something. I would have abided by her wishes but she kept saying, "Whatever you think, doctor."

The ball was in my court and I had to go for it. "The chemo will probably make you very sick, Hilda, but it is the only chance. Dr. Dolan wants to start the chemo tomorrow, but before he does so, he wants you to receive some blood. Your blood is very low and we need to get that up before the chemo starts tomorrow. We are going to start the blood this evening and it will finish by early morning. OK?"

She smiled and said, "Whatever you think, doctor." She had become so frail, so fast. She looked child-like, dwarfed by the pillows. She smiled sweetly as she said good-by.

The next morning, I was making my rounds early and I couldn't find Hilda's chart. "Hilda died during the night," said a nurse.

"She seemed fine at 3; breathing and sleeping just as good as you or I. Then when we went back about an hour later – she was dead. We didn't want to bother you, so we called the doctor-on-call"

I always wanted them to call me if one of my patients died. At least the dreaded call to the family informing them of a loved one's passing would be from someone they knew instead of a total stranger. Or worse still, I feared entering the hospital to make rounds, meeting a family member, telling them I was just about to go up and see so-and-so, and hearing them say, "Oh, don't you know? He or she died!"

I was too shocked to admonish the nurses for not calling me. I had not expected Hilda to die that night, maybe next week but not last night. There had been no signs. I had to make that dreaded phone call – the nurse had already done so – but I should offer any help I could to the family and express my sympathy.

I said, "Don (her son), sorry about Hilda. I didn't expect it or I would have called you last evening. Probably for the better, she would have suffered with the chemo. Apparently she passed away peacefully in her sleep."

"Doc, Art died."

"Whaa!"

"Last night. We didn't call you; the doctor-on-call pronounced him. He stopped eating since Hilda went into hospital. He was getting weaker but he seemed fine when we put him to bed. He died around midnight."

I suspect Hilda and Art are still having their ice cream, on the hill, overlooking the bay.

*   *   *

I remember one afternoon, lying in my bed, looking out the window. There are some tall pine trees bordering the property of Stan Cassidy. I stared at these pines, enjoying their majestic appearance against the sky, when a crow happened to alight on a branch high up. I watched him skip from branch to branch. So effortless! His brain, so small, yet he performed manoeuvres I could only dream of. I couldn't even lift my hand. These lessons in humility are so hard. I continued to stare at him, half mad that I should be envious of a crow, and half enthralled with how marvellous nature can be. Did I take these things for granted before?

Reality hit one day. *'I am locked in! I had a brainstem stroke! I may not improve! I could be like this for the rest of my life!'*

This was reality. *'I'm not at summer camp. I won't return to work in September. I probably won't return to work – ever!'*

Reality hit hard.

I fought the rising panic by thinking of Don, who was dying with cancer. Paula, Ken, Joe, particularly sick patients I had left in Saint John. Their reality was bleak too – I was not alone.

I thought of what I would do with my practice. Would I sell it? It seemed so final, like I was abandoning all hope. I needed time.

I clung to hope. Hope that I would walk out of there. *'I'm young. I can beat this thing.'*

Once reality struck, anger was not long behind but it did not last. I had the benefit of being a doctor for twenty years. I had seen good people struck down by disease and die for no good reason. I hated cancer. Despite trying my best to screen for cancer, it still happened. I listened carefully to complaints, trying to hear the symptoms of cancer whispering to me. I did screening tests that weren't even popular. Still the sneaky disease beat me.

I thought of Pauli dying of Scleroderma, Don with cancer of the lung, Pat with Alzheimer's, and many more who were dying as I lay there. I saw before my eyes so many who had passed away over the twenty years. Ron, such a gentle soul, yet he developed metastatic cancer to his brain and in his last days behaved completely out of character. It made it so hard for his family. So many deaths, so many ways to die; the memories of my deceased patients and their courage saved me from anger, gave me strength.

Instead of 'why me?' I quickly realized, 'why not me?' Why would I think I was so special as to be spared calamity? I was never angry with God. I had long ago come to the conclusion that God has no direct involvement in the day-to-day affairs of man. That was the only way I could make sense of children dying, cancer, motor vehicle accidents, rapes, and other misfortunes. There may be a higher purpose to all the tragedies of mankind but I can not understand.

Thus I went through denial, quickly through anger and 'why me?' stages, lingered briefly in the 'what ifs', and quietly arrived at acceptance. With acceptance, depression came. The depression was appropriate; how could anyone not become depressed? There are things I will never be able to do – activities I loved. I mourned my losses.

I never became clinically depressed – although that is very common after a stroke. I felt 'blue'. This depression manifested itself one bright, sparkling, June morning.

*   *   *

It was a Saturday, a bright glorious day and the nursing staff got me up and into my wheelchair. I felt miserable as I often did on beautiful days. Jill decided to wheel me outside for some fresh air. I saw a reflection of myself in the glass door on the way out. It was hard to imagine that that was I. I didn't feel like that poor creature reflected in the mirror. Staring back at me was someone with the same blonde hair, but with no expression on his face. *I am smiling, am I not?* His head is back, held up by a headrest. He has a tube coming out of his throat with a white bandage around it. He wears my T-shirt and shorts but with white, tight stockings up past the leggings of his shorts. His abdomen is protuberant – larger than I have. My appearance only added to my sadness.

The air felt good as we wheeled out the sliding doors. She took me around the front, down the side of the building to the deck of the Kiwanis House. It was already hot for 10 A.M. The birds were singing, the leaves were rustling, the insects were humming, and the more glorious the day, the more I drifted into despair. I wanted so badly at that moment to be free, to stand up, to run amongst the trees, to lie down on the grass, to be free of this body. I couldn't imagine spending the rest of my life like this.

When we settled on the deck, I made a motion with my eyes that I wanted to tell Jill something. Through the eye gaze board I said, "Please kill me."

Jill was shocked and said with tears in her eyes, "Don't even think it!"

"Not now" I spelled. "No improvement – twelve months." Although I felt like ending my life right then, I would give it more time. I had thought about it and I didn't wish to live my life like this: unable to move either arm or leg, unable to smile, speak, eat – partake of life.

I thought of how I would commit suicide. It would be impossible if I couldn't move; I would need help. Jill couldn't actively help me. Perhaps I could refuse the tube feedings.

A year later I read about Jim, a man in his forties who suffered a brainstem stroke. His wife interacted with us – brainstem stroke survivors – through the Internet. She told us of their struggles from the time he had the stroke. Despite therapy, he didn't improve, and after months he decided to end his life by stopping the tube feedings.

My spirit constantly wanted to be free; is it a sin to set it free? I don't know, but I do know I would have chosen death rather than life like that. I expect I wouldn't have waited twelve months with no improvement before I asked for the tube feedings to stop.

Jill tells me now that I wasn't crying that day, even though my emotions were quite labile when I asked the question of assisted suicide. Jill, looking away, crying, said, "Yes."

I could tell she didn't mean it. She just said 'yes' to shut me up. I meant what I said, but I realized it was too soon, much too soon, for her to comprehend. I thought I would approach the subject later. I felt so sorry for Jill.

*   *   *

I never had to bring up the subject again because I started to improve. First my left thumb moved, then my fingers, my neck got stronger; I showed signs of progression. I expected this rate of recovery to continue. I was still 'locked in' – none of the movements were functional – but I replaced hopelessness with hope.

As I approach my two-year anniversary of living as a disabled person, I still have hope. Hope I may yet walk; hope I may yet use my right arm; hope I may talk better. I cling to that hope. I realize I may never walk but I keep trying – I am improving – Who knows? Without hope, you'll stop trying, and for sure you won't improve. Hope doesn't hurt anyone as long as it's not masking reality.

I am getting ahead of myself but I wanted to impress upon you, the reader, how important hope was, and still is, in my recovery. June was a month of emotions as I settled into Stan Cassidy and got used to the idea of being a disabled person.

*   *   *

June is the month Father's Day is celebrated. I had tears as my children presented me with gifts. They made me cards, which said the sweetest things. They knew my emotions were labile so they didn't lay it on too thick. I felt bad for them when I cried; it must be traumatic for children to see their Dad cry. Jill prepared them well. She told them that I really couldn't help crying; it was a side effect of the stroke. My children seemed to be able to discount my emotions and not be affected by them. I have Jill to thank for this, as I do for so many things.

Colin, our twenty-year-old son, brought my dog up to see me. Jenny is an eight-year-old Miniature German Schnauzer. I am quite fond of her and there is no doubt who her master is. I groomed her, took her for walks, played with her, and I was the one who usually fed her. We had a favourite route for our walks and a special area where I let her off the leash and she went into the woods, did her 'thing', and then came back. I found these walks enjoyable, therapeutic, and a way to unwind from a busy day.

I was afraid to see her. I envisaged a scene: Jenny jumping for joy at seeing me and I crying in front of everyone. People who are standing around in front of Stan Cassidy seeing this grown man crying over a little dog. Jenny would be jumping up on my lap, licking my face, glad to have me back.

I needn't have worried. Colin parked on the far side of the parking lot so I could be away from people. As I approached, she watched me motoring towards her in the power chair. She didn't jump for joy, run to me, or even wag her tail. She looked at me and then through me. Her eyes glazed and she resumed sniffing the ground, occasionally greeting Jill or my kids, but pretending I didn't exist. In a curious way it was a relief. It spared me the pain and tears a joyful greeting would have brought. It was easier to say 'good bye'. I still cried; in fact I cried before I even saw her, anticipating the scene. I understood when her eyes glazed over.

Months before my stroke, I read the book *The Hidden Life of Dogs* by Elizabeth Marshall Thomas. She describes how the domesticated dog retains a fair amount of his natural, wild, pack dog behaviour. She reported that a group of domestic dogs quickly reverted to the social behaviour of wild pack dogs when left on their own. They had a leader – the alpha – whom they all obeyed. She surmised that a solitary dog treats the human family like a pack. Someone becomes the alpha, the leader whom they obey and respect. Dogs do not want to be the alpha but they will assume the role if need be. A good example of why you need to be firm but loving with your dog – if a dog assumes the role of alpha, watch out!

I expect I was the alpha in Jenny's world. The alpha has responsibilities, at the very least to be around to protect the pack. If the alpha is disgraced by another dog or by not doing his duties, he is ostracized by the pack. He is not 'seen' by the others – he becomes a lone wolf. In Jenny's eyes, by suddenly vanishing from the family and turning up here, I am a disgrace. I went from alpha to lone wolf as her eyes glazed over.

This I understood. There was no doubt she knew who I was; her sense of smell is keen. Yet I am in a wheelchair – a contraption she has never seen – I am breathing through a tube in my throat – I make no sound to greet her – I don't pat her, play with her, or use my arms – I don't even smile. How is she to react? Perhaps she doesn't know? Perhaps she doesn't understand? It is all too confusing to her so she reacts the only way she knows how: she ignores the whole situation. She pretends I don't even exist until she can make some sense of it.

I don't know if Jenny's reaction was a normal, canine, social reaction or confusion or a combination of both, but two years after the event she is just now warming up to me. Jill has supplanted me as her alpha. She has accepted the wheelchair but she doesn't like it. She doesn't understand or refuses to recognize my voice, probably because I sound gruff with little variation in pitch. I don't mind; it's nice just to be accepted back into her pack.

*   *   *

As I've already alluded, emotions were hard to control. I cried over everything: letters, cards, friends, Jill leaving, Jill coming, it didn't matter – I cried. I felt embarrassed if I cried in front of people.

In one incident, I cried in front of an assembly of staff. Dwight

Allaby and Eric Ross had been at the Centre for a long time. They had progressed to the point where they were being discharged. All staff and patients gathered in the cafeteria in a big circle. When the speeches of farewell were said, I burst into tears. Luckily I couldn't make a sound, but I was ashamed of the tears streaming down my face.

Another time my Mom and stepfather, Ron, decided it would be good for me to get out of Stan Cassidy for a while. They brought up a war movie and we went over to Kiwanis House to watch it. I cried seeing men being killed. Crying over a war movie!

I knew the staff was used to emotional labiality in post-stroke patients. I was used to it in my own practice. But not I! *I am a doctor. I council people with tears, through tragedies, through deaths; I haven't cried in years.* I knew it was foolish to think this way, but I couldn't help feeling others think it is a sign of weakness.

The emotional turmoil goes away, slowly. Nobody can say when or if it will leave, but it takes many months. It was a relief to finally gain control. For me it was perhaps the worst thing about this stroke. Foolish pride!

I wish I could cry now. It was a good release. A good cry would feel better than anger and frustration. Damn testosterone, socialization, gender development or whatever!

I cried whenever Jill had to leave for Saint John. I knew she had to go: she had business to attend to, my children needed her, and besides, she had nowhere to stay, the Kiwanis was often full. It didn't matter; I cried when I knew she had to leave. My mom and stepfather tried to fill the void by staying near when Jill was absent.

I am ashamed because I know I made it harder for Jill to leave me. It was tough for Jill to see me cry, but if she could only have seen me a few minutes later, I was fine. My friend, Barbie, often came in to sit with me and we watched reruns of 'Seinfeld'. Jill was afraid I might need someone and couldn't ring the bell. I could move the left thumb, so when she left she placed the call bell in my left hand so I could buzz for attention.

There is one night I am especially ashamed of. It was a Sunday evening. The kids had spent the weekend at our cottage. My parents have a cottage close to mine, so I knew the kids were fine and enjoying themselves. They later told me they liked the responsibility of looking after the cottage. I think they appreciated the fact that we trusted them.

Jill was heading home for a few days. The day had been sunny. I normally would have been heading back to the city after spending a weekend at the cottage, but the reality was I'm here. I wished so much to be going home with Jill. I suddenly missed my kids, my cottage, driving – freedom. I felt trapped. I wanted out – anywhere. *It's not fair!* As Jill – with tears in her eyes – was about to leave, I made matters worse by motioning with my left arm that I wanted to slash my wrist. I felt anger but tears were streaming down my face. I felt I had no control of my body, my desires, and my emotions. I wanted Jill to feel my pain.

I am so ashamed of my irrational actions when I think of it now. Jill hated to leave me and I compounded the problem. I eventually got hold of myself and tried to stop crying by immersing myself in a TV program. I realized I was acting foolish but I was still angry. We talked it out like always and once I was able to 'verbalize' my feelings, I felt relief.

After awhile, Barbie came in to keep me company. The tears were gone and I enjoyed her conversation. When she left, I continued to stare at the TV, not aware of what was on – thinking of what had just occurred, of life, and feeling sorry for myself. Soon the nurses came in, prepared me for bed, and gave me that sweet sleeping pill – welcomed so that I may stop thinking and slip away.

Most stroke victims feel anger at some point. You can only be accepting so long. Eventually frustration or a feeling of unfairness boils over. You have been wronged and someone is going to hear about it! Unfortunately it is often the one you love. Marriages break up after stroke. Some people never get over their anger and constantly blame their spouse for being well. *Nobody owes me anything; I have a choice: self- pity/anger or moving on. Channel that wasted energy from anger to physical exertion, Shawn. Remember bad things happen – they just do. Get on with it.*

I have the advantage of being a family doctor, so I have been involved in counselling post-stroke victims and families. However, anger still crept into me. I suppose it was OK. I let it happen, I dealt with it, and moved on. I tried to remind myself: Jill was not to blame for being well and she had a life to live, don't begrudge her that.

*   *   *

The support I received surprised me. I did not expect it from my colleagues. One afternoon Dr. Mike Morse came to visit me. I thought it was nice of him to have come so far. I was astounded at what he had to tell me: "At a medical society meeting, we have decided to get Jill an apartment – here in Fredericton – so she won't have to travel back and forth. Don't worry about the cost. We will look after that. I have an appointment in a little while to look at one for her. It's just down the hill. OK?"

I was shocked. If my mouth had been capable of opening up, he would have seen a man impersonating a fish. I did not cry. I was too amazed for that. I've always been a private person, and I found it hard to accept such generosity. But it will be so nice to have Jill nearby.

I later learned my colleagues donated money to a fund, and had a dinner and dance, as a fund-raiser for me. Bill Tait, Dr. Mike Morse and his wife Beatrice spearheaded the dance. I learned to accept gifts, humbly and gratefully, as there will be many more, during my long convalescence.

CHAPTER 7 – JULY

Having Jill nearby was a blessing. I didn't have to worry about her driving from Saint John and it boosted my spirits when she arrived at physiotherapy each morning.

In July, the heat continued. I was usually decked out in T-shirt, shorts, sneakers, and of course, my beautiful white anti-embolic stockings. I was still in my private room because of my trach care, tube feedings, and the high level nursing care I required.

I got out more now because I graduated to a power chair. I could move my left arm enough to steer. Doreen (OT) put my forearm in an armrest that controls the chair. To make it go forward, I pressed down; backwards, up; right inward; left outward. The outward motion or external rotation of the forearm was the hardest motion for me to get. The paralysed arm liked to stay curled up into the body. The arm protested any attempt to move it otherwise.

I spent many hours going around in circles. If I relaxed for a second, the arm tone brought the arm control in and I started to spin. I practised manoeuvring my chair in the parking lot. I was much more careful inside, although I have left my mark on Stan Cassidy's walls.

I had to be placed in my seat like an astronaut. And in fact, it did take a team of nurses to do it, but I was free. I felt independent being able to read the schedule board and head down on my own. The schedule board listed our names, days of the week, and when each therapy was scheduled for each individual. When I wanted to go for a breath of fresh air, I went out the main doors – which opened automatically – by myself. Fresh air when you want it! It sounds so basic, but what a treat.

Before the power chair (don't say electric! That makes me nervous!) I was dependent upon the nursing staff or Jill for transportation. I couldn't thank Doreen enough for this newfound freedom.

I saw fellow patients more. Interact is not the right word here; I eavesdropped upon their conversations. There was a wide assortment of injuries, diseases, and ages. I looked quite a sight but I didn't feel out of place. We limped, wheeled, swore inappropriately, laughed, and cried – we did it all.

We were all facing major changes in our lives – some more than others – but the attitude that prevailed in Stan Cassidy was positive. It could have been a sad place, a place of broken lives, tears, but instead there was hope and love. Don't get the wrong impression; there was tragedy, frustration, tears, broken hearts, and anger, but the staff never let the mood become sombre.

I enjoyed interacting with my fellow patients. I listened, laughed by coughing up gobs of phlegm out of my trach at some joke, and then usually ended my 'conversation' by farting. Oh, I was quite the social butterfly!

It was so hard to converse. By the time I spelled out my joke about something that was said, the conversation had moved on to another topic and my joke was received with puzzlement! Never try to tell a joke with an eye gaze board.

I was never shunned. The patients always made room for me. I tried my best to turn away when I laughed or they might get a gob of phlegm flying their way. They didn't know it but I talked with them the whole time. I thought I was very funny.

I wanted very much to talk with my fellow patients. 'Misery loves company'. I wanted to ask them things that only patients would understand. How was their day going? *I feel miserable. I couldn't lift my left hand up to my chest. I did that yesterday. Mereille is so nice to me – how's Carly to work with? Isn't it a pain to have to go to bed so early! How are you sleeping by the way?*

It would be enjoyable to commiserate with someone – to share feelings. By being 'locked in', I was locked out. I was alone with my thoughts and feelings. Thank God I had Jill. I asked her to ask my fellow patients questions. Just because I am a doctor doesn't mean I 'know it all'. I've never been on this side of the fence before.

I wanted to discuss feelings with someone besides Jill. How were they coping? Did they have bad days too? Jill got it all and even at that it was superficial because of my communication problem. I have a new appreciation for the deaf and the mute and problems they must encounter. If you are 'locked out', I hope you have someone who knows you are still 'in there', and still need to talk.

We are social animals; communication in some form is essential. I missed it – big time! Even to be able to wave a 'hello', nod, or smile in passing would have been a relief. Having a Coke, talking about the weather, small talk within a group – how I longed for interaction!

I am a quiet fellow; always have been and especially now, always will be. It is perhaps appropriate that I should get this malady. I was always shy growing up and later when I grew out of this shyness, others always seemed to say it better than I. I made up for this quietness at home. I joked, played my guitar, sang, and talked all the time. My children's impression of me is probably far different than my colleagues'. I don't think I appreciated how devastating the effects of aphasic (talking) problems were in stroke victims.

Socialization was fair using Jill as my go between but communication with the nursing staff continued to be tedious. Most staff had little knowledge of the eye gaze board and they continued to point to each letter. I felt perhaps they could have held an in-service, to instruct the staff on how to communicate with me. It was simple and fast to learn.

I had to give the nurses credit though; no matter how busy they were, most tried to understand what I was saying. Doreen and Beth explored all manner of communicative devices with me. They chose these devices depending upon my ability. For example, at one point I gained movement back in my neck so that I could move my head from side to side. Big button-type buzzers were hung on either side of my headrest. I was to learn Morse code, and then, through a computer, I would be able to talk. Thankfully I moved beyond this point of ability within two weeks as my left hand improved. Now I attempted a similar method, only with my hand.

I tried one weekend to learn Morse code, but my heart wasn't in it. *As soon as they get this trach out, I'm going to talk. Damn it! What was the point of wasting so much energy learning Morse code?*

They were trying to utilize what ability I had at any given moment in a functional way. I knew that. Yet I balked. Doreen put a device on my forehead that moved a cursor on a computer. I thought it was all very interesting but also very disheartening. *I won't need this; I'm improving far beyond this!*

I was scared they thought this was it. I tried to be a good boy and act interested but I was thinking, *No way, José! These instruments are for disabled people!*

Disability was hard to accept. Inside, I felt the same. I didn't feel disabled. It was hard to accept that I was disabled. Besides, some people said this condition would continue to improve. Yes, but there has to be a time we say, "Well, I guess that's it!" Isn't there?

I would then accept it (or try to) and move on. There is a difference between acceptance and giving up. Just because I accept that I won't walk doesn't mean I have abandoned hope that some-day I will walk. This is a question that tormented me: Does the acceptance of reality stop possible progression? If I doubt my ability to walk, will it prevent me from obtaining that goal? If I say, "I will walk!" does it increase my chances?

* * *

It was hard to always fail in physiotherapy. I couldn't do too much. Mereille asked me to sit up on the side of the exercise mat.

Betty, the physio assistant, and Mereille manipulated me into a sitting position. My spine was bent over like I was ready to roll forward; I was expending a huge amount of energy just trying to keep my head up and my legs were giving me no support on the floor. My balance was nonexistent. Mereille said, "Straighten your back, Shawn."

I barely perceived a movement. "Gooda!" exclaimed Mereille.

I let out a whoosh-squeak through my trach. I barely perceived a movement and Mereille says it's, "Gooda!"

This scene repeated itself throughout my stay, Mereille would say, "Gooda!" at some small achievement and I would laugh. I'm glad they thought it was laughter because sometimes it was a cry. When I achieved some small goal, I felt like crying for joy. I felt like crying for bending back my left wrist another inch, for bending my knee, for many small movements. I was so desperate for any small improvement – a sign that I was becoming 'normal'. *Let them think I'm laughing at Mereille's exuberance; it's less embarrassing this way.*

The gymnasium where physio took place was huge. There were two big rooms and unlike the rest of the Centre, it was modern and had the best of equipment. There were lots of windows, bright colours, and many smiles. Energy circulated around the room with machines whirling, encouragements being shouted, and laughter.

Mereille chose a blue mat with a steel mesh platform over it. It would be 'my mat' for the next ten months. It was electronic; they could raise or lower it by foot pedals. On a wall adjacent to the mat was a poster of whales out in a bay. It became my focus for tranquility.

I eventually did master some semblance of sitting without looking like a rag doll. This meant I progressed from a Hoyer Lift for transfers to a sliding board.

The Hoyer Lift is a device used by nursing staff to transfer patients from bed to wheelchair and vice versa without manually lifting the patient. The sensation of swinging through the air is exactly like the feeling you get on a swing. I did not like the sensation in the least. I never complained – after all what could they do? – But there did seem to be nurses who delighted in giving me an extra spin. I was scared of heights as it was and this experience did nothing to alleviate this phobia. In fact, my phobia seemed to get worse; I would get a peculiar sensation in the pit of my stomach when they showed shots from high angles on TV.

I got bed baths most of the time, but later I graduated to tub baths. I was brought to the bath perched precariously, like a baby being carried in a stork's beak, down the corridor, stark naked, all the while trying to smile. I was covered in a blanket, but I knew, and anyone I met knew, I was naked underneath. It was hard to keep up appearances while dangling in the air naked.

The bathroom was big enough for the tub, a nurse on both sides, and no more. It was a tricky manoeuvre to get the Hoyer Lift and me through the narrow doorway and into the bath, all the while preserving my dignity. The tub itself had a whirlpool feature that I couldn't use, because of my trach. The nurses only forgot once and turned on the whirlpool. They quickly saw the error as my eyes widened in terror, the water bubbling precariously close to my trach.

In the bath, two nurses scrubbed me furiously from either side. I was completely at their mercy. My trach was just above the water line while my arms and legs floated uselessly just below the surface. Yet I never felt anxious. The nursing staff had earned my confidence long ago.

After the bath I took another ride on the Hoyer Lift to dry off in my room. So I was 'Hoyered' in and out of bed, onto my exercise mat and off, and into my bath. When I entertained the thought of writing an account of my journey, I thought I might call it, *Life on the Hoyer Lift*, sort of in the vein of Mark Twain's *Life on the Mississippi*.

I had to find some humour in my life, otherwise it was pretty sad. The Hoyer Lift reminded me of how dependent I had become on machines and people just to do the simplest of tasks. Luckily under Mereille and Doreen's guidance, I graduated to the sliding board.

The sliding board is simply a highly polished board that bridges the gap between two objects, so you can slide across. One might learn to do this independently, but not I! I was no star on this either. I didn't have enough mobility in my trunk, enough strength in my arms, or maybe I had too much lead in my bottom, to accomplish this. In the months I used this technique, I always required people to help me slide along.

The sliding board enabled me to enjoy another activity: going for a car ride. Doreen took me for a short car ride soon after I came to the Centre, but I was hardly able to keep my head up so I didn't enjoy the experience. Now I had better head control and I was eager to try again.

Charlie Love was an assistant in OT who loved to joke around. He told us his alter persona was 'Charlene' because he or she was pretty handy with a sewing machine. Charlie was always humorous and he always had a story to tell. He was a perfect employee for Stan Cassidy. I wished I could have laughed with him instead of spitting at him!

Charlie took Jill and me for my first long car ride. I did all right, at least I got through without needing to have my trach suctioned. I was a little nauseated but I didn't tell them – I had reasons for keeping quiet about it. I wanted to go home. The weekends were driving me crazy.

I mourned the things I had lost and by this time, I knew I had lost them. I loved getting up early Saturday morning, doing my rounds at the hospital, and then coming back home to start my chores. I loved working around my home or cottage; finishing tasks gave me a sense of accomplishment. I knew I would never be capable of doing most everyday jobs. (I may learn to walk but I will be very unsteady.)

I continued to wake up early and one Saturday I woke up to a glorious sunny day. It was about 5:30 when I awoke and the room was already heating up from the sun pouring in the windows. The air conditioner had been on all night but it was unable to keep up to the sun's heat that morning. I became uncomfortable with the heat and struggled with the call bell. They opened the window wider for me, and at my request turned on the TV.

I was not interested in what was on – and I didn't have the ability to change the channels – but I wanted some relief from my thoughts. I'd be at the cottage – *Let's see what needs to be done – the deck needs stain in a few areas – got to plant those new plants I purchased – got to fix that bank by the back of the house – boat needs a good scrubbing. Wait! I can't do these things! I will never be able to do these things!* I tortured myself with negative thoughts. I wanted so desperately to do something with my hands to take my mind off things. *Get up! Get busy!*

An hour went by – two hours. A nurse came in to start my tube feeding. *Great, I'll be here another two hours!* Think! Think! Think! That's all I could do. Jill was away. I didn't have her to talk to. I didn't think of it, at the time, but I should have had a talking book available for these times.

It was now four hours since I had been awoken. I wanted to do something. I wanted to move – stop thinking – I wanted to feel the air – I wanted to…. I didn't know… I wanted to swing my legs out of this bed and walk! I got frustrated. I grew angry with every-one. *No one knows what this is like!*

The nurses stopped my tube feedings and told me they would be back. I waited another hour. Thinking, thinking – the cartoons on TV irritated me and made me feel sad because I had no way to turn them off. I was reduced to watching them on a Saturday morning instead of being out in the sun. I wanted to yell – move. I felt trapped.

When the nurses finally did come, they started to bathe me

and prepare me for the day. I started to cry. I had cried before over silly things like a war movie, but this was the first time I had cried over my condition to anyone other than Jill. The nurse explained they thought by letting me sleep in on a Saturday morning they were doing me a favour.

I couldn't stay mad at them, but when they placed me outside the front door, I felt depressed. The day was glorious and I couldn't enjoy it. I had wasted over five hours – doing nothing! I felt hurt – this wasn't fair! *I don't deserve this! I was always kind. I never intentionally hurt anyone. I helped out others. I tried to be a good Christian. I loved God and my neighbour. I wanted to grow old – see grandchildren – bounce them on my knee – throw them up in the air – make them laugh. Now they will see this figure that can't hold them and doesn't smile. Hard to love that! Why? Why? Why?*

My parents came after awhile and found me sitting outside in a dark mood. I told them how frustrated I was from the morning. I did not tell them how depressed I was; they would feel miserable, making me feel all the more miserable. Besides, I just didn't want to talk about it. I felt better by the afternoon, probably from the social interaction. That morning made me anxious to leave on the weekends. *If I could only get home for two days, I could hack five days here.*

Thus the car ride with Charlie and not telling them I was nauseated. I started to plan and get Jill used to the idea. She was naturally afraid of the responsibility of my care. There was my trach care, tube feedings, transfers, turning during the night, and a lot of things to consider.

Jill accepted the challenge because she knew how desperately I wanted to leave on the weekends. I can never thank her enough. Throughout our marriage, she has always been good to me. We love each other. It did not surprise me that she was willing to try. She was a nurse and this greatly facilitated the learning process. The nurses showed her how to suction my trach, keep it clean, use the infusion pump for my feeds, and transfer me.

Planning for my homecoming kept me happy. It was something to do; finally something active, positive, something to look forward to. Patti, my nurse friend, arranged the nursing schedule for me at home. I needed nurses at night to turn me, clean my trach, and watch me. Jill couldn't possibly do this twenty-four hours a day.

The nurses at Stan Cassidy encouraged us and tried to allay any fears Jill might have. I was not the least bit afraid; I had complete confidence in Jill. I understood the pressure she must feel, having me home, alone – all the scenarios that could happen – but I needed to go home. I was lucky I had a wife who was a nurse; there was room in my home for a rented hospital bed, an infusion pump, a suction machine, and there was insurance for nursing help.

We had lists of all the paraphernalia we would need at home: infusion pump, suction catheters, condom catheters, cans of tube feed, incontinent pads, and much more. The Centre supplied us with the infusion pump and suction machine, on loan. Finally after weeks of planning, we were ready.

Our little car was loaded down and we were followed with more equipment by Louise, the head nurse, and Karen Dickinson, an OT, who took over my care during Doreen's vacation. Meanwhile, I looked like a dead man who was made up to look like a live one. Pillows were placed on either side of me and behind my head to keep me upright – my sunglasses were on, and I still had no expression on my face. It amused me to think of what I must look like to other drivers – something out of a horror story.

The nurses were afraid I might need suctioning in the car, so we took an emergency portable suction along with us. Luckily I never needed it. It felt so normal to be in a car, watching the scenery pass me by, yet at the same time it felt so exciting and new after two months of institutionalization. The trip from Fredericton to Saint John passes through a huge army training ground, Camp Gagetown. There are miles of uninhabited forest. It takes about one and a half hours and without the ability to converse, my mind drifted....

* * *

Great lessons are learned in the practice of medicine. I learned from almost every encounter, dealing with human life, emotions, and tragedies. Some of these lessons were painful. One of my most painful lessons involved Steve.

Steve owned his own business and was moderately successful. I saw him often because he had hypertension that was hard to control, and insomnia. His insomnia was the worst case I had ever encountered. I tried the entire regular non-pharmaceutical remedies, all the hypnotics, mild tranquilizers, psychological methods – everything. Although he didn't seem depressed, I thought it might be atypical or masked – so we tried antidepressants. I had consulted him to psychiatrists, psychologists, neurologists, and any specialty I could think of, however remote the possibility. Nothing helped!

Hence, I saw him often. Somehow he maintained a good sense of humour throughout his ordeal and we had a good doctor – patient relationship. We did not have sleep laboratories at that time. He would have been a fascinating candidate.

At some point Steve came into the office with a sore ankle. The x-rays and blood work revealed nothing. It kept getting worse despite anti-inflammatory drugs (drugs for arthritis) and local treatments. A bone scan of the ankle revealed nothing. I was perplexed but not worried – he had no other symptoms – so I sent him to a rheumatoid specialist. In the meantime, I was going on vacation and had a locum tremens (a doctor who, for short periods, takes over a practice) relieving me.

I had a great time on my vacation until the final week. My locum phoned me with bad news. She told me I would probably want to know that Steve has been admitted and he has wide-spread cancer. Apparently Steve presented to the Emergency Dept. with bad chest pain. The x-ray was suspicious and the total bone scan confirmed he had widespread cancer in his bones. There was hardly an area that was spared – most unusual. The news hit me right in the stomach. I was numb.

I struggled through the rest of my vacation, trying to act jolly for the family, but my mind was elsewhere. Sleep came poorly as I poured over each office visit in my mind. What had I missed? I had done a localized bone scan because it was cheaper and I could get it faster – if only I had done a total scan! After going over everything, I was convinced I had not missed anything. He never complained of any other pain or symptoms. Besides, the ankle pain was probably metastasis (cancer had spread) and it was probably too late then anyway. Why hadn't my x-rays and localized bone scan shown anything?

I drove myself crazy, tormented myself with self-doubts. Regardless of whether I had or had not done a good job, I knew it did not look too good in the eyes of the layperson. It looked like I had completely misdiagnosed it. I suppose I had, but with the information I was presented with, I had done my best.

His wife was not my patient. She did not know me. I anticipated that she would be angry and suspicious of me. I used to feel hurt when people sometimes showed their anger towards me when a loved one was dying. But later I grew to realize that anger is a normal stage of grieving. Every doctor has to learn to accept or understand the anger directed towards him or her, even if it is inappropriate. If people can be angry with God over a loved one dying, I should not be surprised they could be angry with the doctor.

She was better than I expected. She acted a little confrontational but who wouldn't? I was anxious about this meeting, about seeing Steve, and time was going – always that time factor! I had to get to the office. So I wasn't really listening when I heard her say, "Whatever you do, don't tell him what he's got!"

I heard and I didn't hear. I was moving into his room and I just nodded. After I had greeted Steve and asked him to tell me what happened, how his symptoms were, how they were treating him (he was under internal medicine service – not me) he got out of bed and sat in a chair beside me.

He stared into my eyes and asked me, "What's wrong with me?"

I realized what I had just said to his wife. I had never lied to a patient before. Most of the literature on death and dying states that you should be open and frank with a dying patient. The unknown is more frightening than knowing. I have always tried to answer a patient's question truthfully but leave them with some hope. I don't give them bleak forecasts (even if it is) if not asked.

That moment is forever frozen in time for me, like the little girl's face in the car I nearly hit that got me into this mess. I felt the eyes of Steve's wife glaring at me from behind Steve. I felt Steve's eyes searching my eyes, imploring me for the truth. I told him.

That scene plays over and over in my mind ever since then. It has been over ten years since Steve died and I still wonder: Was I right to tell him? I've come to the conclusion – no. Every dying patient has the right to know and his eyes seemed to be saying that he was frantic for the truth. I think someone should have told him – but not me. I went against her wishes and I should have respected them. When she told me her wish – not to tell him his diagnosis – I should have listened, taken my time and explained my position. But no, I was in too big a hurry and too anxious. If she didn't agree with me – about the dying having the right to know – I should have never gone into the room.

Since I wasn't the attending physician, I could have told him, "I can't answer that. You'll have to ask Dr. ____." But that smells like a cop-out to me. I have seen too many 'pass the buck' answers happen in hospitals. A patient can leave hospital not knowing exactly what has transpired. However, maybe in this instance, if I had wanted to see Steve, it would have been the best option.

I was wrong. I learned to always, always – no matter how tired I am, how rushed, how bored – to always listen to what is being said to me. Not only patients – anyone. If I don't have time – tough – take time.

Steve's autopsy never revealed the primary tumour. His body was riddled with adenocarcinoma but they were all small metastases. I spoke to the pathologist and he assured me he looked everywhere carefully. I suspect renal (kidney) as the primary site. No matter where the primary site was, it must have been very small, probably too small to cause symptoms.

It is very unusual for a small tumour to be disseminated so widely in the body. Something was drastically wrong with Steve's immune system. Sleep is needed for the body to repair itself; I have often wondered if Steve's immune system was compromised because of his terrible insomnia. Who knows?

*   *   *

It felt strange approaching my home; I felt like a kid returning home after a prolonged summer vacation. Jill had had a ramp built around the side of my home, onto the deck. On the deck, our friends had decorated the railings with balloons and welcome home signs. A lump in my throat grew, and when I entered the back door and saw the fireplace, tears started to come down. I felt foolish in front of the girls but for the first time I had some control in preventing all-out bawling. Karen and Louise quickly got things in place, assessed that I would be safe, and left.

Alone – for the first time in over two months. There were no nurses or doctors around. I was quietly ecstatic! The day was cloudy and foggy, so I didn't spend too long on my deck but it was the first place I went. Later I glanced up the stairs to my bedroom. The bedroom is large with an attached bathroom that has a whirlpool. I expected to be able to ascend those stairs one of these days. I envisioned going up the stairs backwards, on my behind, lifting up with my arms. My left arm was coming, I expected my right arm to follow suit.

Jill rented a hospital bed for me and set it up in our living room. I eventually rested and had my tube feeding. The kids arrived home from school and a few of my friends came. The company over the next few weekends was steady, maybe tiresome, but a good thing; they kept me from thinking too much about my situation and wallowing in self-pity.

I had to accept the nurses I required at night if I was to continue to come home. I wanted to shut the door at night and be with Jill and my children, by myself, like old times. I accepted reality. I had to. *Step by step – no matter how small – accept – lucky to be home,* I told myself. Nurses watched me in my room while I slept. It didn't bother me because I had my magic little sleeping pill. I was gone, oblivious to my surroundings.

I hated needing someone else, a stranger in my home, only because it reminded me how disabled I had become. I was dependant on others to defecate, urinate, eat, and breathe. And yet I felt like the same Shawn. My hope was that my disability would be temporary. My private duty nurses were all great. Patti covered any time a shift couldn't be filled, and the weekends at home made my time at Stan Cassidy more tolerable. Being home didn't make everything all 'peachy'. Far from it. It reminded me of all the things I missed.

The next morning I cried with Jill. After the morning wash up, Jill wheeled me out to the breakfast table. My breakfast nook looks out onto our backyard, via bay windows. The woods were active with birds despite the rather foggy day; a good day to do those chores that needed to be done inside the house, or curl up with a book on the sofa.

The realization that my life had changed hit me hard. *This may not be a transient stage – this may be it! I may never be able to get out of this chair! I can't even curl up and read a book on the sofa.*

I was overcome with the feeling of being confined to the wheelchair. I felt trapped! It wasn't even that comfortable. My behind was already starting to cry out for relief. I didn't want to go back to bed so soon! *What am I going to do with the rest of the day? I want to move!*

I hung my head and cried; big tears – deep sorrow – frustration – grey colours. I was thankful my kids weren't up but, as usual, poor Jill became my emotional washcloth. It was hard to express emotion through an eye gaze board but I told her, I'm just frustrated. Jill cried with me and told me it *isn't* fair. For not the first time she tells me I didn't deserve it.

I didn't deserve this! This reminds me that Pauli didn't deserve the Scleroderma, Dorothy didn't deserve her cancer, Susan didn't deserve her MS – I am reminded again that it is not a question of who deserves what? I am not special; it just happens. I read a book by Kushner many years ago, *Why Bad Things Happen to Good People.* It helped me make sense of tragedy involving my patients and I think it helped me during these times.

My poor wife had to listen to these emotional outbursts. We are too close for my emotions not to affect her. I realize this but cannot help it. The stroke survivor's partner has a heavy load to bear. They have to deal with emotional outbursts and maybe personality changes on top of increased physical demands. The stroke survivor may not act like the same person they married. Usually by the time a stroke occurs the marriage has been firmly established, yet more than 50% of them end in divorce after a stroke.

My emotional outbursts quickly resolved and made me feel better. The rest of the day was spent in visits from friends, resting in bed, watching TV, and 'talking' to my kids and Jill. Leaving later in the day for Fredericton was especially painful. My kids helped me into the car, sliding me along my board. Not a simple task, but once accomplished I left them in the driveway. And as we pulled out, I already missed them. Colin, acting so mature at the age of twenty, watching out for his sisters. Beth such a gentle soul, in her last year of high school – is she able to concentrate on her schoolwork? Tara, in Grade 8; she will have to get up tomorrow, eat breakfast by herself, and go to school. I felt so guilty and sad seeing my children waving good-bye; I burst into tears.

I'm supposed to be the strong one – helping my kids and they're helping me. They're smiling and waving good-bye and I'm the one crying. Stop it! Stop it! I wanted to stop crying but I had no control. I didn't want my children to see me like this. I felt stupid. Jill handed me a tissue and I gradually got control.

My first day back I quickly became immersed in the daily routine at Stan Cassidy: up shortly after 7am, a quick wash up and tube feed, and Beth comes in for my swallowing exercises at 9. It is good that one is kept busy at Stan Cassidy – less time for thinking. But I was still aching to socialize.

Later in the week, as one of the nurses washed me in bed, on the radio I heard of a twenty-nine-year-old girl who had died in a motor vehicle accident on the highway. The news reinforced my view of being an unfortunate victim of circumstance. I didn't *deserve* it, but neither did that twenty-nine-year-old girl who just died. At least I was living.

Another phrase occurred to me at around this time: *Shit happens!* Those young men in Viet Nam could not have summed it up better. It was the only way they could make sense of the mayhem back then. I will use that phrase for myself and to others when they ask me how I feel about what happened. That about sums it up. It prevented me from dwelling on negative thoughts, 'what ifs', anger, and self-pity: *Shit does happen!* It just does, man. *Shit happens!*

* * *

Entertaining things happen with the nursing staff sometimes. Kim is a small girl who works like a hummingbird. It's like she's taken an overdose of thyroid medication before each shift. She does not walk; she runs from task to task. I have never seen this girl saunter. She is strong despite her small stature. She pulls me across my sliding board with minimal effort. She easily lifts me up from lying to sitting position. Larger nurses find this a hard task, especially because of my rigidity, but little Kim, all seventy or eighty pounds of her, finds it no problem at all.

One morning it was her turn to suction my tracheostomy and clean it. They were trying not to suction and humidify my trach as often, to see if it would dry up and give me a solid night's sleep. I had spent quite a good night, and for the first time I did get through the night with no suctioning or humidity, but they had given me some moist air just before Kim came in. This is given to keep the mucous moist and prevent it from drying out.

I breathed quietly, but as I found out, it was 'the quiet before the storm'. The phlegm dried out during the night but there was just as much; it just didn't gurgle as much.

Kim talked about how nice it was out, her dog, and her husband Jack. She quickly arranged her trach tray, attached the suction tube to the suction machine, turned the noisy thing on and dove in.

It worked, she created a cough and she quickly removed the tube with only a small amount of mucous. "This is curious," Kim said. "You always produce more phlegm than this. You went all night; perhaps we missed it. I'll go down again."

The first cough had produced little mucous but an ominous noise like the rumblings of a volcano before it erupts. I heard and felt it. I was about to spew the mother of all hawkers.

Kim took careful aim, intent on her mission: suction up those goobers or die trying. The sun streamed into my room, making the room close with heat. Kim had her mask on. I imagined it to be hot for her. I remembered times in the Operating Room when I was involved in an especially long procedure; each breath seemed hotter as you re-breathed the air that didn't escape the mask. How good that first breath was outside the OR when you took off the mask.

I watched as Kim leaned over my trach tube. *Don't do that!* I wanted to yell. Once in the Emergency Room a girl came in with an apparent drug overdose. It apparently hadn't happened that long ago because we elected to do a gastric lavage, hoping to get some pills up before they absorbed. I inserted a large gastric tube down her throat and then poured water down the tube. By pressing on her stomach, we expected the contents would soon follow. Nothing happened. We turned her on her side and pressed harder - nothing. I added more water to her gastric contents, pressed again – nothing. Pressed harder – nothing. Remember Elmer Fudd looking down his gun barrel when it didn't fire? Remember what happened to him! I obviously learned nothing from this lesson as a youngster. What I hoped to see – I have no idea – but see something I did! As I looked down the barrel (the gastric tube) peering for that mysterious obstruction, the girl decided to vomit up her pre-suicidal meal. Why would someone contemplating suicide decide to eat ham and eggs before they overdosed? And a good quantity too!

I stood there with partially digested ham and eggs over my head and clothes while the nurses roared. However I had managed to lavage most of the pills, along with the ham and eggs, and the patient lived to eat more ham and eggs. My dignity was not so lucky.

I thought of this as Kim precariously worked over my trach. This time her suctioning worked! But it was too copious and too thick for a measly suction tube. My cough reflex worked just fine and I ejected more phlegm than I thought humanly possible. Kim held her ground – fine nurse that she is – and took the full disgorgement of my night's rest. My lungs had been quite active that night, for Kim was covered – her face, glasses, and hair. She continued to work on me and only cleaned off her face when the necessary tasks were finished.

Kim's hair, however, was lambasted with gobs of phlegm. She did not seem to be aware of this as she finished cleaning me up. I was afraid that at any minute an emergency call bell would ring in another patient's room and off she would rush, mindless of her hair looking like she crawled out of someone's nightmare!

I tried to point to her hair, but my left arm didn't elevate satisfactorily and I ended up pointing towards the washroom. After another question and blink the eyes session, we finally communicated that she should look at her hair.

Kim was not freaked out as she looked in the mirror, "Oh that's alright; it happens."

She finished my care calmly and later washed her hair. But I noticed after this that she held her head back whenever she did my trach care – sensible girl! Maybe she didn't understand the lesson Elmer Fudd gave us either!

*　　*　　*

My world was still fuzzy, compounding my feelings of unreality. My eyes were not synchronized – diplopia – I was still seeing double. Eric Ross, the brainstem stroke survivor who was a year ahead of me in recovery, still had double vision. I started to worry that double vision might be my fate also. Eric and I both wore an eye patch over one eye to stop the double vision. I found the patch hot and I wore it infrequently, preferring the diplopia rather than the heat and sweat.

Each morning on awakening I looked at my room number on my door. Double '8's – I knew nothing had changed. I hoped one day I would awake and find my legs and arms moving. One morning I would greet Louise, or some other nurse, at the door as they made their morning rounds. "Good morning!" I'd say.

They would cover their mouths, astonished, and they would scream, "Shawn, whaa?" Then they'd laugh and we would all cry. I'd thank them all, walk to physio, repeat the scene with Mereille, Doreen, and Beth, go back to my room, pack my bags for home while waiting for Dr. Milczarek (mill-chair-ik). I knew it would never happen but you can't help dreaming.

One morning the 8's seemed closer together. I looked at the clock; it seemed better. Imagination? If improvement had occurred, the rest of the day wasn't as convincing.

The next day the 8's seemed closer still, and within a matter of a week my vision was normal. By the time I went home the next weekend I saw the forest clearly. *That was an osprey nest on the electrical tower near Welsford! The clouds were so clear in the blue sky!* I smiled all the way home that weekend, although you couldn't tell by my expression.

I thought, *all recovery will be like this and maybe, just maybe, I'm on my way. Each week now something else will improve! Perhaps next week my left arm, and then the week after – my left leg, and then...*

No function ever improved as rapidly as my eyes did. Stroke can be cruel during the recovery phase. Sometimes improvement can be a tease; you can't duplicate the achievement, or if you can, it is weeks later. Sometimes gains are painfully slow; huge amounts of energy are expended for small gains. It is frustrating, heart-breaking work, and you never know if all the work will bear fruit. You can't give up! I work every day; it's been two years and there are still improvements!

It is hard to exercise some days. There have been no improvements for weeks and you feel there is no point continuing. Then some function improves – you move your arm a little further – and all that work has meant something. That's how it goes. Then when should you stop? I guess when those little rewards stop. When is that? I don't know. I don't think anyone can tell you. If your doctor or therapist stops your physio or OT, it doesn't mean you stop at home. They are just saying the amount of care they are giving you isn't appropriate for the small gains you are getting. There are other people they have to see who may benefit more from their treatment. They are not telling you to stop. Don't give up until the little man inside your head tells you to. And even then, question him and make sure he's not just tired.

Besides, activities at home are a form of therapy. I have to remind myself of that over and over. Jill wants to help me, out of kindness, and it is tempting to allow her to. Getting the cap off the toothpaste may seem like small potatoes, but it's therapy. If you want to rehabilitate to your full potential – don't get lazy!

* * *

Beth came in twice a day. She concentrated on my swallow. I swallowed reflexively but not on command, certainly not good enough for eating. Not even good enough to swallow my own saliva. I hated being in bed but at least I didn't drool. When I went out to the lounge, I was aware of my drooling and how I must appear. I didn't have just a polite stream of drool out of my mouth but a whole river!

I was very aware then of how disabled I must appear to strangers. A brain-injured, poor man, unable to move anything, no expression on his face, drooling at the mouth... 'Isn't it nice how his family takes him out and talks to him like he's normal.'

I felt so normal inside that I had to remind myself the person they saw **was** I. The only thing they got wrong was – I wasn't brain-injured. I felt strangers looking at me – wondering. I wanted to scream at them, *I'm normal! I'm a doctor! I have children! Two months ago I walked, drove, played guitar, golfed* (badly) *and sang* (badly again). *I could talk to you about sports, politics, bananas – whatever!* Instead I offered them no reaction; I stared and drooled with little expression. If they looked closely, they may have seen my eyes tearing over as I read their minds.

I tried not to dwell on what people thought, nor did I care what they thought: I was getting better. This was only a temporary station.

The drooling was so bad it soaked my shirt within a half hour. My chin would get sore and irritated from the saliva contact. I got so exasperated with the condition I literally 'put a sock in it'. I requested my family to stuff a towel in my mouth to soak up the saliva. If I thought I looked bad before – I now, definitely, warranted a second look!

My poor mother stared at me in disbelief when I first asked her to stuff a towel in my mouth. Mom and Dad had just wheeled me out to the lounge to watch TV on the big screen. After awhile, tired again of my constant drool, I made my request to Mom through the eye-gaze board. She was not a 'star' on using the board and I could see she thought she made a mistake. "Ron (my father)! You see what he's saying? I'm so stupid with this."

Resigning myself to the inevitable, I repeated myself on the board to Dad. "Well, I think he said, 'put a towel in my mouth."

"That's what I thought you said!" Mom exclaimed. " You want me to put a towel in your mouth?"

How strange this request must seem to her strikes me, and I begin to laugh-cough.

"Why in God's name would someone want a towel shoved in their mouth?" Mom laughs.

Somehow I manage between coughing fits to explain my strange request. A towel is procured and placed in my mouth. Mom does not want to hurt me and I end up with only a corner of the towel in my mouth, but not wanting to confuse anyone further, I sit satisfied.

One evening as I sat watching TV with a towel stuffed in my mouth, Pierre, a motor vehicle accident victim who had been in a coma for six months, came into the lounge. One arm and leg were severely crippled and his good side was not great. His mouth was twisted and he spoke with a drunk-like drawl. He was hard to make out but he said, "Can I watch the weather for a second?"

Gee, the poor guy – must have had quite a crack-up – looks bad – must have lost a few marbles from that one! So thinks the boy with a towel sticking out his mouth! A great one to prejudge. Pierre became my friend. His survival and recovery were remarkable, his tenacity to improve and his outlook on life – inspiring. And best of all his humour made me choke on more than one occasion. This was the last time I ever prejudged anyone, based on his or her first appearance.

I would have been only too glad to get rid of the towel. So I approached my sessions with Beth with great interest. She placed cold objects in the back of my mouth hoping to induce a swallow. Usually nothing happened; progress was slow. After weeks of this I started to produce a voluntary weak swallow. Now I tried to do it on command. Beth would place her hand on my throat and ask me to swallow. I don't even think I can do a swallow on command now! There seemed to be a psychological block and I became afraid they wouldn't let me eat until I could swallow on command.

It was a great source of frustration for me. I tried to close my eyes and imagine drinking water but nothing helped. After weeks – I did get better but never mastered the technique – Beth asked me to try to swallow twice within a certain time span. It was hard and it took a long time and a lot of practice but eventually I did it, to Beth's satisfaction.

Along with these swallowing exercises, Beth also spent time trying to get my facial muscles working. She asked me to frown, smile, pucker and round my lips. At first there was no movement – it seemed impossible. But eventually with time and Beth's persistence, movement occurred. Unfortunately and usually, the stroke survivor obtains no sudden achievement and thus no positive reinforcement.

There was no day I screamed, "I can move it!" I could not perceive the return of movement; it was so gradual. When did I first move my lips? Hard to pinpoint; it happened, but when?

It would have been nice to have a few 'Eureka's'. Most of the goals were achieved without any fanfare. The other day I turned off a light in the bathroom. I never could raise my arm high enough to manipulate that switch before, so I had used an extension attached to it. When did I start raising my arm that high? I have no idea.

Beth tried to induce my facial muscles to work by placing ice on my face over the muscle she wanted to move. Eventually my mouth opened a crack and I was amazed to find my tongue did not work. The things we take for granted! I could not get my tongue out of my mouth.

Doreen kept changing the controls on the power chair to challenge my left hand. She stretched my hands and exercised them. Finally my left hand started to move. We spent time making a fist, releasing the grip, and trying to pinch with the index finger and thumb. Every step was hard but it was worth it. I made progress. I could see the improvements week by week. No 'Eureka's!' but steady.

One day Doreen had me pick up, with my left hand, little plastic mice from one container and place them in another. It was a Thursday morning. I remembered that on Thursday mornings I often did minor surgery. In fact the day of my whiplash I had just removed a basal cell carcinoma from a man's face.

My left hand refused to cooperate. If I managed to raise my hand high enough to grasp the mice, it took all my strength to move my arm over and let go. In my frustration, I thought of how easy it had been to remove that basal cell just two months ago, and now I couldn't move stupid plastic mice! Those mice depressed me. I hated their stupid tails, bright colours, and plastic smell. I begrudged bright, sunny, summer days while I sat in this therapy room trying – and usually failing – to pick up plastic mice. I realized how important those mice were. I didn't really hate them. But it was hard. It was hard to not feel sorry for myself when I wanted to be golfing, swimming, boating, working – anything on this nice day. I fought this emotion. I did not want to feel sorry for myself. *It's just tough luck! Remember – shit happens – Shawn! More people than you are not able to enjoy summer days.*

In physiotherapy, Mereille concentrated on my sitting balance and posture. Often I went on a tilt table; while you are strapped on, the table is gradually tilted to an upright position. People can get quite dizzy when first using it, but I, thankfully, never had this problem. As I got closer to ninety degrees, the feeling of falling forward increased. I knew I was perfectly OK, but that knowledge didn't stop the terror.

It was good for me to experience weight on my feet. I started to move my left arm and hand up towards my face. At first there was only the ability to move my arm to my waist; then my belly, then weeks later, my chest. My right arm showed no inclination to move.

It was on the tilt table that my legs had the first signs of movement. Mereille had me bend my knees and then, using my thigh muscles, come back up again. It was a struggle; my thighs burned. Mereille asked me to go lower. *I can't do it,* I thought. But down I went to the verge of collapse and back up I struggled. Physiotherapy is hard work – nothing comes easy – failure is common. I wanted to be normal so bad I welcomed this scheduled torture – for as long as they could take me.

Actually, I never found physiotherapy a torture. It was hard – yes – but never torturous. Mereille was always cheerful and encouraging. I became dependant on her, and demonstrated this one-day.

Mereille's vacation time was due. I was about to lose Mereille for three weeks. Of course, I knew everyone has vacation and naturally I would be sad to see her go, but in my emotionally labile state – I cried. Horrors! Right in the gym, in front of everyone, Dr. Jennings decides to bawl his eyes out. I know, I know, everyone knows about stroke and emotional fragility, especially in this centre – but this is me!

I knew Mereille understood, but I felt humiliated. Nothing made me feel more abnormal than crying. I quickly left the gym, and no sooner was I out the door, the crying stopped.

*   *   *

Dr. Milczarek usually visited me in the mornings before my therapies started. He always took time, sat down and always tried to understand me. He was another one who knew how to use the eye gaze board, so I could talk to him. My main concern was getting the trach out and removing the peg tube from my stomach.

When? When? was my main question. Of course it was hard for him to say, or perhaps he didn't want me to hear the truth. I thought in terms of weeks, and he probably knew, months. He was a tall, average build fellow, with dark curly hair and a moustache. At first he seemed very serious, probably because I seemed serious – it is hard to joke using an eye-gaze board. Later when I could talk, I found him very friendly and approachable about any of my concerns.

He wasn't a 'hands on' type of doctor; I think he relied on reports from Mereille and Doreen at Case Conference, which they held once a week and when they talked about every patient. He always knew how I was progressing, but up to this point he seemed evasive in answering my questions.

One morning in July, he was very frank; he told me I probably wouldn't learn to walk! I looked at him and nodded. I probably looked like I took this news very calmly, but I was aided by my expressionless face; inside, my stomach knotted, my heart missed a beat, and my emotions froze. My somewhat good mood tumbled down and I was looking reality in the face again.

I didn't like what I saw. I didn't believe I could live in a wheelchair – it was too uncomfortable, too confining. *He doesn't know me. I've always fought back. I've been able to achieve anything, if I put my mind to it. I've never failed. What he is saying is probably true – most people in my position probably wouldn't learn to walk. I will!*

Dr. Milczarek later told me – based upon my progress up to that point – he thought walking was an unlikely achievement. I am thankful he was always honest with me, but at that time I convinced myself that he told me the worst-case scenario. *He probably didn't want me getting false hopes. I am a physician; I know how we work.*

The sinking feeling didn't last long. I felt I would improve at a quicker pace once the trach was removed. I requested and obtained scientific studies on brainstem strokes from Dr. Milczarek. The news wasn't good.

Most brainstem stroke victims died. Of those that did survive, the majority maintained a fair degree of disability. A small number regained normal function. I noticed the average age of the brainstem stroke patients tended to be younger than those with cerebral stroke, which is by far the most common type.

The hope of complete recovery dwindled but I thought, *maybe I'll be somewhere in between. At least I'll walk.*

* * *

Nurses had to do everything for me. Having another person wipe my eyes was difficult; they usually wiped too softly. It is hard for anyone to gauge how hard or soft to wipe an eye. Later in the day, the sleep from my eyes would fall back in or dissolve, giving me an intense burning.

Another difficulty was where to place the call bell? At least now I could use one. It was a large button type of bell that had to be pressed. Usually they pinned it on my pillow and I had to turn my head. The problem was, sometimes I slid down during the night because the head of my bed was elevated to help me breathe and I couldn't reach the bell. I spent a good many hours uncomfortable, wanting to turn, or wet because my condom catheter slipped off, or in some other discomfort.

One night in particular was uncomfortable – I woke up with vomitus in my mouth. I felt ill and retched again but not all the vomitus came up; it stayed in my throat. I had a hard time trying to bring it up or swallow, and it was burning. It was one night they had deflated the trach (deflated the air bulb that holds the trach in place in my trachea) so I was scared I might aspirate.

When I tried to call the nurse, I found the call bell was now above my head. I tried wiggling my head to bring the bell down but the pillow didn't budge. I could make no sound with my arms or legs. I blew out my trach as hard as I could, hoping a sound would be created, but my attempts were feeble due to my small lung capacity. I couldn't cough on demand – I tried but nothing came.

I continued to be nauseated and thought I might vomit at any time, heightening my fear of aspiration. The burning in my throat and mouth continued. I was alone – no roommate. It was the only time I was ever frightened at the Centre. I spent a good hour in this state – lying in my own vomitus, trying to swallow, afraid I might vomit again, and trying to make a sound. Finally a nurse came on her regular rounds.

Later I became able to move my left hand enough to press the bell. Later still I had enough strength in my left thumb to use a regular call bell if it was pinned nearby. The above situation was never repeated but those first two months were difficult. I hope a better system to call for help for the "locked in" patient is available or can be devised in the future.

* * *

Slowly a condition that became my main obstacle to rehabilitation, my main source of pain, my heartbreak, came – rigidity. It started so slowly I barely noticed.

When an injury occurs to the spinal cord, no messages get to the muscles. The lower motor neurons (nerve cells in the spinal cord that connect directly to specific muscles) tell that muscle to turn on. For an unknown reason, some muscles are turned on more than others; the result is the arms tend to be flexed (bent at the elbow and held into the body) and the legs extended (straight and held together).

They started to stretch me every morning before physio. Some movements were painful, some were not so bad, but all are very necessary. I am still stretched every morning. It has become as routine as brushing my teeth. It is hard on my wife, so three times a week I have a nursing assistant who comes in and performs the exercises.

Betty is a physiotherapy assistant who became my friend. Every morning she came in and stretched my arms and legs. At first this occurred in my room after breakfast, and later in the gym just before my physiotherapy. Everyday, weekends included, Betty or Jill did it.

I grew fond of Betty. We communicated somehow and I learned about her family and she mine. Betty was middle-aged with a grown up family and a husband, Ed, who developed a heart problem during my stay. My word to describe Betty would be gentle. It is hard to stretch someone to the point of pain and still describe them as gentle but that was Betty. Again, I wish I could have talked better, but we did all right.

A few months later, when we started to do the stretches in the gym, Esmond joined us. (The exercises took quite a lot of time and to shorten the activity we started to perform the stretching with two people at the same time.) Esmond was a middle-aged well-built fellow with white hair, who was always smiling. He worked as an assistant in physiotherapy, occupational therapy, and recreation. He

amused me with his tales of horses, home, cars, and past experiences. He always had a story and was always cheerful. Esmond
took one leg and Betty the other and off they would go; we called it
synchronized physiotherapy!

As July came to a close, I had not progressed as far as I had
expected. But I still had hope that I would pick up once the trach
and the feeding tube were removed. Maybe soon?

CHAPTER 8 – AUGUST

In August the hot weather persisted. I was still the fashion boy in my white stockings and shorts. I continued to breath through my neck and was nourished via the stomach tube.

The hot weather teased me into thinking about water. My glass of water would have ice cubes poured from a big glass pitcher, with moisture beads clinging to the outside. The imagery made my throat quiver in anticipation.

After tormenting myself with this vision, the thing I most wanted was Coke. I don't know why. I'm not a big Coke drinker but I desperately wanted a drink of Coke. I suppose it was the wetness, coldness, fizz, and taste – the whole sensation at once. I missed the sensation of taste and the act of chewing. My dietician, Sharon Cameron, presented me with ice cubes made from Coke, and allowed me a small amount. They didn't trust me with ice cubes, and for that reason I liked speech therapy sessions because Beth often used ice cubes to help me swallow.

Besides thirst, bugs were another torment during the summer. If a fly happened to enter my room, I could count on a few moments of fun; or if there was only one fly in the whole building, he found me when my tube feeding started.

They landed on my face (usually my nose, as it is quite prominent!) and took a little walk-about. This being most annoying, I tried shaking them off with my head, which I could do slowly by this time. This bothered the timid ones but had no effect on most flies. They liked to look in my nostrils, but thankfully they are basically cowards and no one ventured in.

Around this time, I had a dream that a fly went down my trach into my throat, laid eggs, and later out came a writhing mass of maggots! I guess my little unwanted guests were affecting me. They landed on my feeding tube, looking for a way in. They crawled along my bare arms, tickling me. Unable to swat them, I was helpless – a big playground for flies. Jill bought two fly swatters and kept guard. The nurses became expert marksmen on my behalf.

It sounds like the Centre must have been dirty, but that was far from the truth. The flies got in because of the two large sets of doors at the entrance that opened automatically, and they were always opening and closing. There were not many flies; they just all seemed to like me and told all their friends, "Hey, there's a guy in there who doesn't mind us taking a walk-about. C'mon!"

Flies were harmless, but the black-flies and mosquitoes were not! Outside I was fair game. A mosquito would land on my arm and I was helpless. I watched as they chose their site, then filled their bellies with my blood. Word soon got around among them too! Jill would catch me flashing my eyes for help but it was often too late.

Worse than the mosquitoes were the black-flies in June. Those suckers hurt! And worse again were the horseflies. They elicited a most vigorous shake of the head and often a 'whoosh' sound from my trach – my 'May Day! May Day!' warning. Then there were the "creepy-crawlies' – harmless for the most part, but bent on making nightmares real. A spider crawled up my white stockings, up my leg, disappearing under my shorts never to be seen again. I'm assuming that after he had a bit of fun at my expense, he left. I felt helpless; if any insect chose to explore my body, he had free reign until seen by Jill. Often some creepy varmint took a shortcut up the wheelchair and onto my arm. If an insect landed on the back of my neck, it was bad – I couldn't see what it was and I didn't know if they crawled under my shirt or flew away. I didn't like what I could not see.

I was never afraid of insects when I was able-bodied and had the option of picking them off. I was not so brave now – now that I was an insect amusement park.

* * *

August was my month of impatience; the routine of hospital life, my slow progress, my inability to eat, and my trach all frustrated me.

My trach did not behave. Louise had deflated the cuff that surrounds the tube and holds it in place in the trachea. Deflating proved that I was not aspirating mucus from my throat, yet I contended it caused another problem: every time I moved, the tube moved in my airway and I coughed. I felt my coughing was slowing my progress; each time I tried to turn or bend, a coughing spasm struck. My trachea seemed especially sensitive. They were waiting for my trachea to settle down and produce less mucous; they expected it to dry up. It never did – I continued to expectorate until they removed the tube.

I had to demonstrate that I could breath with the trach corked or covered. I lasted a breath or two the first time before I sent the cap flying across the room. I failed each time, and when Louise would indicate that that was enough for today, I was mad at myself. I thought I could do it. Another failure! I wanted the trach removed so badly. I thought I would start talking, eating; maybe even improve physically. Presto! I hoped the removal of my trach was the key to instant improvement. If stroke rehabilitation were only so easy. I knew the truth but I chose to hope for an easy way out.

I was sure I could talk without the trach. The words were right there in my head and Sandy (my neurologist friend) had said my speech centre was spared. When Louise capped my trach the first time and asked me to speak, I was shocked. I said, "How are you?" but out came a feeble, "aaah".

No matter – I'm just out of practice. I did believe this, but the doctor part of me said, *See, I told you so! Why do you keep thinking you're different than any patient you've ever seen!* I guess because I had seen plenty of stroke patients but never a brainstem stroke patient – maybe they were different. Besides, I had no experience as a patient. I walked the walk. I was a patient. I thought like a patient. I *did* leave my black bag in my truck; it only found its way to me on occasion.

I tried to believe the reason for my lack of air support, and my inability to breath around the tube when it was corked, was because my trachea was too narrow. The real reason was because my vital capacity (or the air we use to breathe) was greatly reduced. The muscles of respiration were very weak.

I would have to be patient, practice, and believe that someday I would be able to breathe with my trach capped. It was so impossible to breath around my trach that at first I couldn't imagine ever being able to do so. I was frustrated. Gradually I tolerated the trach being capped for longer periods of time. It took longer than a month, but eventually I was breathing through my nose. One of my happier moments occurred the day Louise took out my tracheotomy tube. I had never grown used to it or the constant suctioning.

I also grew impatient with the feeding tube. The skin entrance of the tube into my stomach became inflamed. I wanted to start eating and I grew tired with my inability to swallow.

Towards the end of August for a two or three-week period I became nauseated with every tube feed. I felt very ill. I felt nauseated about an hour after the tube feed started. I often implored them to stop the feeds early or to skip one altogether. I asked for and received clear fluids only, for a day. I'm sure I drove Sharon crazy because we all know doctors make lousy patients.

I felt like I was being force-fed – trapped in an insolvable situation. I knew I needed the nutrition and that I had no option, but I couldn't take this any more. As soon as the milky concoction started, I knew, soon would follow the bloating, cramps, nausea, sweaty palms and forehead, and nervousness.

I thought it might be dumping syndrome – a condition whereby the stomach empties too fast into the intestine without fully digesting the food. I had no reason for this, and although talked about a lot, it is quite rare.

Perhaps I had an ulcer or reflux? No pain, but I did regurgitate occasionally and it did taste terrible. Possible, but I thought I was nauseated more than expected in reflux disease.

Perhaps my symptoms were psychological? Maybe I became ill by the appearance of the creamy, milk-like, substance? The nurses tried covering the tube feed with a bag but that didn't help. Travis, a student working in recreation, pasted pictures of beautiful young women over the tube feed. That didn't work, although it may have helped my mood!

I wondered if I was depressed; certainly the cyclic nausea made me feel down. A depressed mood is different than a clinical depression – but which one was I? *I have reason to be depressed – my world has turned upside down. Depression is common after strokes. I can't be happy about my situation. I have some other symptoms too: lack of interest and fatigue.*

I decided later that wasn't the problem. I slept quite well (with pills) and between the bouts of nausea, I felt quite well. I decided it was probably irritable bowel syndrome (IBS). It's very common, I've seen many people with it, and I've always had a touch of it. It is not dangerous, there is nothing abnormal in the diagnostic tests, but I found it more disabling than one would think. In life I have been nauseated from food or the flu, but IBS made me feel worse. I have never felt more ill than when my IBS acted up.

IBS is definitely worse when one is anxious, leading many to believe it is a psychological disease. I think in time we will find out it is a neurological disease of the bowel – the nervous system to the bowel is hyperactive, for whatever reason. When one is relaxed, the bowels actually work harder – when one is upset, the bowel activity is weaker or stops altogether, leading many to believe IBS sufferers are anxious types.

It is hard to treat because there are many different remedies (none hugely successful), which usually means there is no cure. I told Dr. Lecky my suspicion (Dr. Milczarek was away) and asked him to prescribe a small dose of anti-cholinergic. This has worked for me in the past, but I must say it has not been very satisfactory for many of my patients. What works for some, does not work for everyone in this disease. I don't know if it was this pill that helped, or time. Maybe I had the flu! I did have some diarrhea during this period. Doctors! Always trying to heal or diagnose their condition! It's hard not to – I do it everyday – it's what I do.

My ability to urinate without a catheter improved. I could tell now when I wanted to urinate but I had urgency. When I needed to go, I needed to go! There'd better be a nurse handy ready to whip my shorts down, then my diapers and….relief! It wasn't critical if I couldn't hold the urge because I had diapers on. But I tried hard to train my bladder.

I found urinating when sitting down difficult – over shorts and a bulky diaper. Often the nurse did not crush the diapers down enough (I assume because she was afraid of crushing some other things of mine!) and the urinal would be pointing skyward. Physics would dictate that the urine would run back onto me. Unable to verbalize my concern or hold my urine any longer, I challenged physics, only to lose every time.

As time elapsed, I got better control and discarded the diapers, but I wasn't confident in my bladder control until the following spring. Until that time I needed the occasional change of pants and suffered the occasional wounded ego. Again illustrating – nothing improves quickly in stroke recovery.

I was frustrated also by my inability to look after my own personal hygiene. I was dependent on the nurses for everything: washing, drying, shaving, brushing my teeth, everything down to genitalia washing and wiping my behind. I was incapable of attempting any of these tasks so I couldn't play 'the grumpy patient' and say, "Here, let me do that!" I had no resources to allow me to act independent, insolent, or difficult.

I did become difficult in one area: the washing of my hair. It seems so petty when I look back on it, but to me it was important. My hair is blonde, thin, and tends to get oily within a day. I wanted my hair washed every morning before I got up. They do this by using a shampoo tray in bed, a clumsy procedure and quite time consuming. The nurses are very busy in the morning, trying to get everyone ready for breakfast at eight, so often they didn't have time to do anything extra. Most often they did give me a shampoo, probably disrupting their time schedule, and if they couldn't, I silently sulked.

It didn't matter if my hair got washed or not – who was I seeing? What did it matter if my hair was a little greasy for a day? I had to admit I had no logical reason for this compulsion, but for more than twenty years it had been my habit to have a shower as soon as I awoke. I think the craving to have my hair washed was my attempt to hold onto something I missed, an attempt to hold onto some normalcy in my life. Everything had changed, nothing was familiar – urinating, having a bowel movement, brushing my teeth, combing my hair, eating, talking – everything. But it really was only hair washing that I fussed about.

The nursing staff must have thought I was vain, and maybe I was! Maybe this self-psychoanalysis is crap, as self-psychoanalysis usually is, but at least it stopped me from bugging the nurses. One nurse in particular would have understood if it was vanity. Louise warned me about her, the first day I came into Stan Cassidy. She told me that there would be a nurse called Linda, who makes the sign of the cross on my chest with my antiperspirant. I never heard of this religious custom before and didn't know what to expect.

Linda, who had this strange habit, was a cute little French-Canadian nurse. I grew fond of her over the months; she amused me. She was very particular as to how her patients were dressed (apparently my colour co-ordination was non-existent) and cleaned up for the day. When I progressed to the point I could shave myself, my initial attempts were poor, and Linda couldn't stand to let me go around like that; she finished the job. It didn't bother me that I wasn't perfectly shaven. I couldn't meet Linda's standards; even when I thought my results were finally acceptable, she shaved more. There was no hair on my face but plenty of razor burn!

Linda's fussiness amused me and her nursing skills impressed me. I asked her how she came to be called 'Linda', a very English name, I thought, for a French girl. Apparently at the time of her birth in the northern part of New Brunswick, it was a common name for French girls. Her smile and spirit helped me through some troubled times.

* * *

Not far behind my frustrations were my worries. Although I had hope for improving, I realized the real possibility of staying severely handicapped. The probability of not being able to practice medicine loomed as a real threat.

A new doctor in the area wanted to buy my equipment. Selling my equipment inferred that I was not returning to practice. It was hard to finally agree to sell. I had spent over twenty years with a stethoscope around my neck or in my pocket. I had sometimes found, to my embarrassment, a stethoscope around my neck in a store. It felt strange not to be wearing a stethoscope, and stranger still to realize I might never use one again.

I was not worried about my office expenses because I had insurance. It paid the rent, Leah's salary (my receptionist) and ongoing office expenses, and my disability insurance had started this month. But doubts nagged me – would there be enough money to meet all my expenses? Did I take into account that I had two kids in college? What was Leah going to do now, if I couldn't return to work? I worried about the costs to renovate my home to make it wheelchair accessible. I didn't vocalize (funny term since I was mute!) my worries to Jill; she had enough problems. I knew it was better to share my worries with someone, but I kept them to myself.

Despite being sick, frustrated, and worried, I remained hopeful – hopeful because I showed weekly signs of improvement. I felt life returning to my left arm; each week I moved my fingers better, my hand up closer to my face or away from my body, in every parameter. My legs were holding me up better. I reached my goals nearly every week, so I was optimistic.

Despite this optimism, I never strayed too far from reality. After all there was Dr. Milczarek's pronouncement doubting my ability to walk. It had been three months since my stroke and I hadn't come far. My brother, Duane, kept saying my right hand was a few weeks behind my left. *More like three months, Duane,* I felt like saying. No, I never lost sight of reality from June or July on, but I had hope.

It had been three months, and that is when the greatest improvement occurs in stroke recovery. But I had reason to hope. I read, or people told me, that brainstem strokes were different from cerebral strokes; the improvement tended to happen over a longer time frame. I hoped my information was correct because I had no experience with a brainstem stroke. I chose to think positively, and so far I had no reason to believe my improvement would stop now.

*   *   *

Frustrations are inherent in all occupations and indeed in all facets of life; we learn to cope. As society demands more from us, as the speed of interactions increases, so do our stress levels. We have to remember: no one is getting off easy. Nurses, teachers, lawyers, housewives, doctors, car mechanics, storeowners, farmers – no one gets a break. I always tried to remember the old saying – 'Walk a mile in my shoes'. I think we need to realize: we all have frustrations and stress, different types, different degrees, but we all have frustrations in our day-to-day lives.

Mine usually involved the business aspect of running a

practice. I trained to be a doctor, yet I also became a small business owner by owning a practice. I tried to be interested in payrolls, deductions, expenditures, benefits, and balance sheets, but I usually passed these tasks off to Jill. I was lucky she actually did it. I called her my office-manager/nurse, paid her a salary and dodged a major frustration. God Bless her – she didn't like it any better than I.

The politics of medicine, in-hospital territory wars, government, doctor relationships – they all frustrated me and I wasn't good at speaking or leading. But I didn't have to speak; there were other doctors much more dynamic than I, who eventually said what I thought. I was a soldier. I would sit on any committee, investigate, or do a study, but not lead.

I found it difficult and frustrating trying to keep abreast of the ever-changing practice of medicine. I loved the study of medicine, keeping current, reading about new studies, but it was hard with a busy, demanding practice. The economics of running a practice got so poor that taking time off for education became difficult.

The actual practice of medicine – the only thing I wanted to do – was smooth. However the majority of diseases were life-style induced and I admit I used to be frustrated by patients not heeding my advice.

I chose not to allow bad lifestyle habits of my patients to bother me. I gave them the facts, and if they chose to ignore them – that was their business. I always lectured those at risk about lack of exercise, smoking, the dangers of eating a high fat diet, or not including more fibre or fruits and vegetables in their diet. I tried to keep up my attack, but I didn't get frustrated when my advice fell on deaf ears – it was their choice. I did my job, and a few did benefit from my advice; that was reward enough.

Cancer frustrated me though. As the saying goes, 'it can be beaten if detected early'. I took it as a challenge to try to detect cancer early, and a defeat if a patient died of cancer. Cancer of the pancreas and ovary were particularly hard to discover early. This is because these organs are deep inside the body and the cancer can metastasize (spread) early, without much in the way of symptoms.

Barbara was an elegant, pretty lady in her fifties who worked as a legal secretary. She was single, I suspect, because she was so devoted to the care of her mother who had severe asthma. Her mother required frequent hospitalizations, aerosols at home, and constant reassurance (this was before the advancements in asthma care we have today). Despite this Mrs. Reasoner lived to a fine old age before succumbing to heart failure.

A few years after her mother died, Barb married a fine fellow who had recently lost his wife to cancer. After such devotion to her mother she deserved a happy life. Their home was located on the edge of the Kennebecasis River with a sandy beach in front. I couldn't imagine a more idyllic setting – she deserved it.

One morning, before lunch, not long after their wedding, she came in to see me complaining of vague lower abdominal cramps. I did a pelvic exam as part of my investigation, in exploring the possible cause of these abdominal pains. I felt my stomach knot up as I palpated her pelvic area. Instead of empty space and a compliant vaginal wall all I could feel was hard fibrous tissue. My rectal exam revealed the same result.

I felt sick as I clicked into my professional mode and reeled off the investigations and consults I would be ordering. I knew this was not good and it wasn't – she had widespread metastatic cancer of the ovary. Eventually I ended up treating her for terminal cancer at that idyllic setting on the river. Her husband, who had only a few months of his life to share with her, looked after her carefully at home with love and with the devotion she deserved until death.

Each time I drove up to their home to look in on Barb, the beautiful surroundings saddened me. She – more than anyone I knew – deserved to be walking on that beach instead of dying. She had spent her life in the inner city; she would have appreciated that big old tree, the waves, the fall sky, the colours, the smells. Where's the fairness? I think her death prompted me to read Harold Kushner's book, *When Bad Things Happen to Good People.*

Even when you think you've done everything right, cancer can rise out of nowhere and bite. Sarah was in her sixties, her husband had died a few years before of emphysema but she had managed to put her grief behind her and was quite active. I remember her always having a smile – eager to laugh.

I performed a breast exam and found nothing alarming. She was due for a routine mammogram, which was performed and reported as negative. The investigations were completed in the spring of that year and I expected not to see her until the following spring. However she returned in September with a red lump on her breast. I thought perhaps it was an abscess at first glance, but it felt solid to touch. Cancer? No! We just checked it out a few months ago – but if it is cancer, it must be early.

It did prove to be cancerous, and despite surgical resection, chemotherapy, and radiation – it got away from us. Sarah died about a year later. I tried to re-live my examination preceding the cancer – I know I was careful! I did not feel anything suspicious! It must have been there! – Or was it? I felt frustrated – I had done everything right and still cancer beat me! I used this story often in the following years to illustrate to women: do not depend upon my yearly breast exam and the mammogram – it is so important that women conduct their own monthly breast exam – they will often detect a troublesome area before I will – cancer can be very aggressive.

I have many more stories about cancer victims but you get the point. Other diseases frustrated me too, but not as much as cancer.

I had gotten used to frustrations in life; I tried not to react with anger but acceptance. The trach, the tube feedings, my lack of progress, and other matters may have been frustrating but I accepted, tolerated, and swore – 'I will improve'.

*   *   *

Near the end of the month, some positive things started to happen. One morning Beth and Doreen took me to the Chalmers Hospital for swallowing tests under radiographic control. I pleased them, but they seemed to indicate that there was room for improvement. I was disappointed when they stopped the tests; I thought it meant more months of tube feed, but I was wrong. Later that week I had my first meal.

I was excited. It was noontime and they took me to the OT kitchen for my meal. This was the last time I ate by myself, for all the patients are expected to eat together in the main cafeteria. This is part of therapy – introducing and normalizing recently disabled people to social situations. I was thankful to be eating alone because I was anxious. Would I be able to swallow? I envisioned choking and food flying across the room onto everyone's meal.

I surprised myself by holding the spoon normally on my first attempt left-handed. However a struggle ensued: lifting my hand up to my mouth while keeping the spoon level was difficult, but eventually, mission accomplished. They placed a bib around my neck and I was ready. Anxiety started to build. My stomach didn't feel hungry but I had never experienced a hunger pain in over three months, so I wasn't concerned. I felt like an athlete in the blocks awaiting the start of a race; I had trained so hard and for so long, and soon the challenge would start. I was determined to succeed but I was ready for failure.

All negative thoughts evaporated from my mind as Sharon brought in my lunch; it was chicken and rice soup, blended, and thickened with breadcrumbs so that it had a very thick consistency. The smell! I actually could smell *real* food. My taste buds have been deprived for three months and I *would not* fail. They adjusted my elbow so it rested high on a table, making it easier to reach my mouth.

I'm surprised I didn't cry as the first spoonful entered my

mouth. The taste! Chicken – salt – it burst in my mouth. I never tasted anything as glorious as this chicken with rice soup. It may not have looked very good, but I was ready to defend it like a dog with his bone if anyone tried to take it from me. Swallowing was achieved with no choking and my stomach gladly accepted my first real food in four months. Beth, Doreen, Sharon, and Jill watched me closely as I happily ate as much they dared give me. Learning to eat again was never easy – frustrating at times – but I was so thankful to be weaning off tube feeds: I never became discouraged.

* * *

Micheline, the recreation director, was anxious for me to attend an outing. Stan Cassidy Centre has a bus for wheelchairs, and twice a week patients are encouraged to go out to an activity with the group. We'd go to a mall, movie, or restaurant. To get out was a treat but it had an important therapeutic function: integrating newly disabled people back into society.

I was aware of this fact and was concerned about delaying my return to society, but I was anxious about harming someone with my missile-prone trach cap. When I coughed or laughed, the trach cap flew in any random direction. I was afraid of hitting someone in the mall. The possibility seemed real enough that I chose not to attempt any trips yet.

I did not hesitate once my trach was removed. I was not afraid of people seeing me – I was curious to experience the reactions that the disabled must receive. Do people stare? Or look out of the corner of their eye? Are they afraid to speak to us?

My first outing was to a mall. I was excited about getting out for an evening; I had been institutionalized for three months. Esmond, the recreational assistant, loaded us onto the bus one evening for our journey. The others made comments about the weather, what they were going to do at the mall, who was going with whom. I listened.

I shared their enthusiasm but could not demonstrate it. I again felt locked out, observing but not actively involved.

I was not anxious as we disembarked on my debut into society; instead I was joyous, a step closer to normalcy. I felt a comradeship with this group of disabled people; some were in power chairs, a few in manual chairs, some walked, and some were just bewildered. A few were old, a few were young, but we shared common experiences and that gave us our bond.

As I entered the mall it occurred to me: I entered it not only as a doctor, husband, and father, but also for the first time as a disabled person. I still was the doctor – husband – father but I had a new identity and the new label overshadowed all the other personae: first and foremost, I was a disabled person. It is not how I saw myself but how others saw me. I knew I was disabled, the denial phase had long gone, but that night amongst all those able-bodied people, I *felt* disabled.

I had not experienced this type of activity in awhile: so many people scurrying to the next shop, talking, laughing, or doing neither but looking straight ahead intent upon their goal – doing what mall-people do. But they were not looking at me! No one glanced my way. I was not as unique as I thought.

Rather than the mall-people looking at me, it was I who looked at them. I was fascinated to see so many people walking with such ease. I studied how they were doing it: *flex the hips, raise the knee – it doesn't have to be very high – so effortless! – Why can't I learn to do that? Attention all K-Mart shoppers – attention all K-Mart shoppers – get down on your knees and be thankful for being able to walk! Do they realize how wonderful it is, to be able to walk?*

Of course not. Did I ever thank God for the gift of walking? No, I didn't think about it, and I realized I had been like the mall-people: I never saw people in wheelchairs. I think we are so conditioned not to stare at anyone who is 'different', that we soon don't

see the wheelchairs. Now that I am in a wheelchair, I am aware of
the other disabled in wheelchairs. There are a lot of us out there! I
obviously did not 'see' them when I was able-bodied.

Children did look however. They are curious and I welcomed
their attention. However most were already indoctrinated by their
parents 'not to stare', and they watched me from the corner of their
eyes. I wanted to talk – I always sang and played with the little folk
in my office in an attempt to ease their anxiety about 'going to the
doctor'. At first my antics with my little patients may have been
contrived but soon it became natural – acting like a child is a delight;
everyone should do it daily. The children of my practice gave me
joy; I hope in some small way I repaid them.

So I was used to children and wanted to interact with them.
But they hid behind their mother's skirts, afraid of this creature that
stared at them with no expression on his face (by this time I could
manage a faint little smile but it was fleeting and pretty pathetic). He
had a hole in his neck and he hardly moved. Perhaps this was the
bogeyman!

I knew how I looked in their eyes, and so, sadly, I tried to
ignore them. But they amazed me more than their parents: they twirled,
they skipped, they jumped up and while in mid-air twirled about and
landed on their feet facing the opposite way. Amazing! Little
movements that I once never thought about or took for granted now
fascinated me. The body's ability to synchronize balance and the
whole assortment of minute movements that must occur in order to
jump and twirl all in one motion became incredible to me. It is true
'you never appreciate what you've got until it's gone'.

So I stared at the mall-people; they ignored me. I have never
encountered rudeness or insensitivity from the able-bodied population.
I had read about it and was ready but it never happened. I have only
received polite gestures, sometimes to a fault. I have never been
ignored by a sales clerk or spoken about like I wasn't there. I have
been spoken down to like I have a mental problem but that was

ignorance, no ill-will intended. Don't assume because a person looks different or talks poorly that they are mentally challenged. Don't assume a person is illiterate because he or she writes like a child. These are the main obstacles in my life: assumptions that other people make about me.

On my first trip I did find some stores impossible for a wheelchair to manoeuvre. I was not surprised to find this type of obstacle even today in our supposedly enlightened age: aisles too small or clothes racks too close together. It doesn't bother me – I don't go in – their loss – they miss my business and like I said, there are more of us wheelchair dependant people than they probably realize. Government legislation says I must have equal access but I don't like shopping anyway – I'll leave that fight to someone to whom it matters.

I left the mall with mixed feelings but overall I was happy: I found no real pain joining society as a disabled person. I had no hang-ups, no phobias; I enjoyed myself and looked forward to my next outing.

*   *   *

Over at physiotherapy things were improving but very slowly. I progressed from standing on the tilt table to standing by myself holding onto a ladder attached to the wall. They placed my hands on a rung as high as they could stretch my rigid arms, gave me a boost while holding onto my weak hands, and I was on my feet.

I didn't feel very confident; my knees wanted to buckle, my thighs screamed with the weight, my hamstrings were cramped, my calves burned, I held on like I was about to fall down a cliff. Mereille asked me to bend my knee, hold it, and then stand back up again. It wasn't hard bending; it was hard to hold it, and it was impossible to straighten the knee. My leg shook under the strain, but with effort it slowly straightened. "Gooda!" shouted Mereille. "Two more!"

What seems impossible sometimes becomes possible with effort and encouragement such as I received from Mereille. It was never easy; advancement was achieved with sweat, and I didn't realize it then but this stage was easy in comparison to later. Rigidity had become my enemy. When I tried to sit, my hips would not bend. I sat as though my back and pelvis were fused together. I could not stick out my behind which prevented me from sitting far back in my wheelchair. This became a major frustration; people had to grab my pants and pull me back in the chair, creating 'wedgies'.

About this time, Mereille had me stand beside the exercise mat with my hands on a bedside table. My balance was poor. I required the assistance of someone to stand, because as soon as I put any effort into it, my tone kicked in, extending my back and pulling me backwards. But eventually I was standing and gained enough strength in my legs that by the end of August Mereille tried me with a walker.

In Occupational Therapy my left hand improved enough to try a computer. Doreen arranged an armrest and key guard to aid me in typing. I took these devices home on the weekends so I could use my computer to send e-mails to friends.

Beth presented me with a small letter board enabling me to spell words with my finger, instead of using the eye-gaze board. This made conversations much easier and less tiresome for me. I could converse using more abstract ideas and therefore explain in greater clarity what I was thinking.

Around this time, by the end of August, with the introduction of the computer assist devices and the letter board, I considered myself no longer 'locked in'. I could converse with most people – with the eye-gaze board I had been limited. I spent over three months in that living hell we call the Locked In state; I will never forget. Lying in bed – thinking – being totally dependant – frustrations – why me? – unreality – thoughts – thinking more – forever thinking – but above it all, overriding everything – love. Love *does* conquer all. Love of

God, love from family and friends and the love Jill and I share. It may sound simplistic and corny but it's true.

Strangers going through a similar experience asked me via the Internet how I got through it? I tried to think of a clever answer, something to inspire them, but I drew a blank. I could have told them clichés like: 'you have to think positive', 'you *will* fail if you don't try', 'think of small gains as major gains', etc. All of them true, but not the real reason for my accepting and working through it. The real reason? – Love. I felt love from God, from people I hardly knew, from patients, friends, my family, my children and Jill. All we ever want, or at least all I ever wanted in this world, was love. I felt such warmth and love from people, that I was satisfied. Love empowered me to overcome any obstacle or wall in my way. Love allowed me to accept any disability that couldn't be overcome. I hope I never forget this lesson.

I'm sure I *will* forget this lesson, as I get frustrated on a day-to-day basis. As my obsessive personality demands things are to be done – *now*. As my children do things different than I would have. I will be successful and happy if I can remember to stay focused on what really matters in life – love. All the rest is secondary.

I remember seeing Lou Gehrig in an old black and white newsreel as he said good-bye to his fans at Yankee Stadium. He knew he was dying of Amyotrophic Lateral Sclerosis and as his fans solemnly listened, he said, "Today I consider myself the luckiest man on earth."

Before I thought, *touching – nice thing to say in front of thousands of fans; he's telling them how much he appreciates their support.* Now I know what he meant: he *did* consider himself the luckiest man on earth. He felt their love, and there is nothing more powerful on earth.

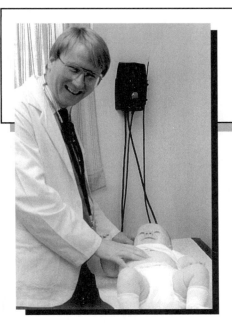

I was happy being a family physician.

Many years ago on the rocks in front of my cottage with the kids.

Todd, Amanda, and Pierre – new friends I made at Stan Cassidy

Trying to learn to walk again using the Lite Gait.

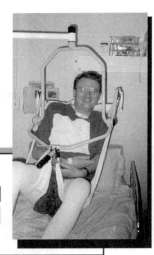

My life on a Hoyer Lift – the only way I could be transferred for months

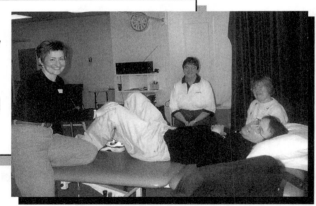

Mereille, Doreen, and Betty, my 'entourage' that took me walking daily

New independence with my power chair

The cottage

At my cottage writing this memoir

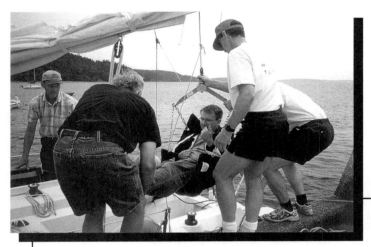

I see possibilities now – not obstacles.
Friends of mine helping me into their boat

It felt good to be back on the river

The welcome home with 100 balloons.

Our family at Beth's graduation.

Patti Nicholson and I giving keynote address at Canadian Association of Occupational Therapists 2002 Conference.

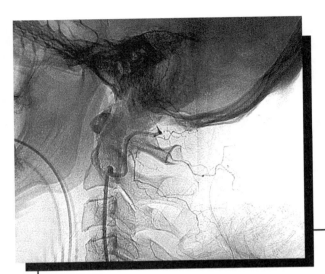

An arteriogram showing my
left vertebral artery blocked

This is my MRI showing the
damage to my brainstem

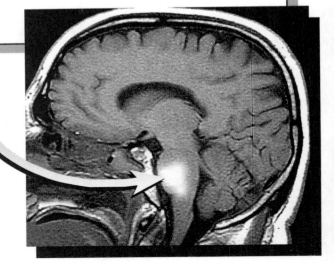

CHAPTER 9 – SEPTEMBER

September always feels like a time of renewal. In New Brunswick, the prevailing winds switch from south or west to the north – colder but fresher. The air of summer has become tired and stagnant and welcomes the new breezes from the north. Later in the season the trees acknowledge this change with a spectacular splash of colour.

September produces a conflict of emotions. The smell of the north in the air promises walks in the country, wearing brightly coloured sweaters, a fireplace burning in the evening, snuggling with a loved one, and the smell of fresh apples. But it also means the loss of songbirds and flowers, summer-swims in the river, and drowsy late-summer afternoons.

I did not recognize the changes as intently that year because I did not experience summer other than the heat; it was my lost summer. I got depressed if I dwelt on it, for I loved the summer: the cottage life, golf, boating, bonfires, and refreshing swims. I missed those experiences but I chose to concentrate on the present – my goals, my rehabilitation, progress – rather than think of the past. I had mourned everything I missed in June and July. I tried to leave that grief behind. It was my choice: wallow in self-pity remembering the past, or live for the present and make the best of it.

Dr. Milczarek gave his consent for the removal of my anti-embolic stockings. I moved my legs enough to prevent clot formation so I no longer needed them. Great timing! The heat of summer had just finished. I was eager to have them removed in any case. Now I needed to work on removing the feeding tube.

The feeding tube bothered me: it was twisting around and irritating my skin; the junction between the peg and the IV tubing kept falling apart during feedings, creating an awful mess. I had to show Sharon I was eating enough, so I ate everything. I made sure I drank high calorie drinks with all of my meals – no matter what they looked like. I coughed and choked everything down, except when I saw Sharon pass by. Then I broke out into a smile as if to say, "This is easy – no sweat – all's cool!"

Beth taught me the correct way to swallow. I had to keep my chin down because I choked if I looked up. My cough reflex was good, so I was never scared of aspirating food into my lungs, but choking is never fun, especially in a cafeteria full of people. A little crumb can be the culprit causing a major coughing spell. Well-meaning people rush over to pat my back as though congratulating me on my superb choking performance. I never wanted to draw attention to myself, but I failed.

I never found pureed food unpalatable. I was so glad to taste anything that I surprised myself by eating everything. Most of it didn't look too good but it tasted fine. However, I would not recommend pureed pancakes – it looks and tastes like the batter before it's cooked. Sharon was fond of saying she could puree anything – yes she can, but is it palatable! Don't try pureed salad! Sharon makes it very presentable; she even purees a tomato, puts it in a mould that looks like a tomato, and places it on top. Disguised or not, the salad tastes like grass. When you combine salad ingredients, mash, chop, and then puree them into an applesauce like consistency, they end up looking like mulched grass and tasting like it too.

Other than these two minor glitches I was surprised how good pureed food can be. My only experience with this type of food was feeding my children when they were babies, and watching my patients in hospital. It was I who often ordered or inflicted this culinary variation upon them. Then I cringed at the thought of ever having to eat this and used to say to Jill, "If I get to the point that I have to eat pureed food – Shoot me!" After September, I never turned my back on Jill!

I must have eaten enough and convinced Sharon, because by the end of September Dr. Milczarek removed the feeding tube. I did not give this up easily; my body must have grown accustomed to it because as he yanked to pop it out (after removing the water in the bulb that kept it in place) my stomach rose with his hand. My abdominal muscles clamped around the tube, angry at losing what they now considered a part of their anatomy. Dr. Milczarek was nothing but determined; he wanted it despite what my abdominal muscles thought. When the spasms in my abdominal muscles calmed down, he braced his left hand against my abdomen, gripped the tube, and pulled.

It took awhile for my abdominal muscles to get over the loss of their friend; they begrudgingly relaxed over the next half hour. I was free! No catheters or tubes – it was all up to me – a major step towards independence. I could now breathe and eat on my own. The rest might come. It might?

* * *

Hope. I still had a lot of hope but it had been four months since my stroke. My speech was a disappointment; I could only make vowel sounds. "Aaaaaa –eeeeeee-iiiiiiii-ooooooo-uuuuuuu." I had started to eat – admittedly food no one else would want. My left hand moved enough to direct my power chair. I needed help to stand, but once up I could stand under my own power. Maybe the first step in walking was around the corner. Maybe.

I continued to be tormented with the dilemma of when I should accept a disability, or should I never accept a disability and keep fighting? It had been four months and my right arm showed very little signs of awakening. My body was rigid, fused together, my back and pelvis moved as one unit. I had very little control over my legs; tone made them stiff, unwilling to participate in my recovery.

I knew by this time that some disability would have to be

accepted. Determination sometimes doesn't win. There is some damage that can't be overcome. I read the statistical outcomes of brainstem stroke; I should be happy just being alive and not staying ' locked in'. Did those people who stayed 'locked in' not have determination? Should we make them feel guilty; inferring they didn't try hard enough? Obviously not. There is some organic damage that can't be overcome, no matter how hard you pray, exercise, or meditate. They are out of luck, until medical science can repair it.

So when should survivors of a brainstem stroke pack it up? Accept our disabilities and learn to live with them? Well, it appears we can continue to show improvement over a number of years. The progress is painfully slow compared to the first three to six months, and you expend far more energy than the results show, but we improve as long as we try. It has to be you or the little man inside you, your intuition, who says, "That's it; too much energy's being wasted for not enough results. I have to get on with life – get a job – find a career – whatever."

I still had hopes of walking. I was unable to picture myself not walking. In my dreams I walked. I felt like a walker. This fellow called Shawn walked. An inner voice called saying, *"No you're not. You are a wheelchair guy. You will always be a wheelchair guy."*

I tried to ignore that voice. I was unwilling to accept it. Dr. Milczarek had told me in July that he didn't think I would learn to walk, but that didn't shake me. I'm a doctor and God knows I've been wrong before. I chose to feel that he was only trying to prepare me, in case I didn't learn to walk. So it was a great shock when Mereille and Doreen told me one September day that I would never walk – at least functionally.

At home on the weekends Jill was making plans for my eventual return home. We had changed our living room to my bedroom and I was sleeping there in a hospital bed that we were renting. It seemed temporary to me; the piano was still by my bed; the formal sofa and curtains as seen in a living room were present also. Besides, where was Jilly? I wanted her beside me. I couldn't conceive of never being with her. I looked up the stairs at our bedroom and assumed that I would be going up those stairs someday. I had still not slept with Jill; I required a nursing assistant to frequently turn me throughout the night. I no longer required a nurse; my days of trach care and tube feedings were over.

When Jill started making plans about remodelling the downstairs bathroom and making it wheelchair accessible with a knocked-out vanity, raised toilet, and shower, I tuned out. I think it was too real, an admission of my disability. The cost to renovate worried me. I was receiving a disability cheque by this time and it covered expenses but that was all. Any extra expense would require a loan. I didn't see how we could afford the payments on another loan (I didn't think of the auto insurance). I should have talked to someone about my concerns – at least Jill, but I didn't want to worry her further.

Jill talked to Doreen about designing the bathroom to make it appropriate for me. Where to put the grab bars? What type of shower? I listened, detached, agreeing to decisions but not really believing this discussion would bear fruit. I was not helping Jill make decisions about renovations. Besides, fellow patients had implored me not to make any hasty changes. They improved and now they were sorry they went through the expense and effort of renovating their homes. I listened to them; a part of me was still holding out for that miracle.

Mereille and Doreen were working on my posture by one of the exercise mats; Jill had just spoken again about the renovations and about the necessity of doing so at this time. Doreen said, "You know, Shawn's never going to walk normal. He will never use your stairs to get up to the bathroom. He will never get up from a chair and just walk to the kitchen."

I watched Mereille's face as Doreen said this; she kept her

head down and worked on my right hand, bending and massaging my stiff muscles. Doreen's face was red and her conversation hurried; she was uncomfortable in having to tell us this.

My stomach tightened with Doreen's forecast and Mereille's silence said enough – *they think I will never walk too! It isn't just Dr. Milczarek's opinion.*

A part of me (probably the doctor part) knew this to be true. But the real me, the real Shawn, hoped for greater things. He hoped to walk out of there. He hoped to be walking the 'old footpath' to Sand Point at his cottage. He hoped to canoe again. He hoped to walk on a beach, lie in the sun, go for a swim. He had been hoping for so many things and they all came crashing down.

I stared at them impassively; I did not cry, which was amazing. I was numb, devoid of feelings, lost in my sorrow; all gone – my dreams, ambitions, and hopes.

This conversation occurred in the morning just before lunch. I didn't have time to recover before going to lunch. I ordered as though nothing had just occurred, but my life had been turned over, altered. I didn't taste the food: my mouth was dry, my throat constricted. I ate mechanically with no thought other than – *no walking- they don't think I can learn – I will never walk – never walk – never walk – never walk.*

Everyone else ate and conversed like nothing had happened. Again I was reminded that life continues, even though a tragedy has occurred in my life, nothing has changed for them.

After lunch I spoke with Jill about what they had said. "Whaa di' you thin' of tha' – wha' Doween sai'."

"I think they said, you won't walk."

"Wha di' thea saa it."

"I don't know."

"Do you bewieve it?"

"I don't know."

I could see Jill was crushed and feeling like me. I had become dependent on Doreen and Mereille and valued their opinion. I knew what they said to be true, but it took some time for me to accept. I now had to toss away my dream of walking normally, but they didn't say, 'I wouldn't walk', and over the ensuing days and weeks, Doreen and Mereille didn't stop ambulating me. In fact, they seemed to be increasing their efforts in helping me walk. I had to change my ambition from walking normally to maybe – maybe someday, taking a few steps with the walker on my own, and then who knows?

I didn't abandon my hopes of normal walking completely. Who knows what medical science may come up with? Researchers are experimenting with stem cells and maybe someday they will be able to inject my brainstem with them, which will differentiate into neurons, and I'll get up from my wheelchair. *They* might? I noticed how it had changed from *I* might? Still…hope.

*   *   *

I had thought about the possibility of never walking again while lying in the NICU. I couldn't fathom the idea of never walking on the rocks that guard the front of my cottage from the river. I built my cottage about five years ago at Buckley's Cove, on the Kingston Peninsula. It is built on a rocky outcrop at the tip of the Peninsula, on the St. John River. It looks across the river to Ingleside, and to the left, Grand Bay, and consequently it bears the full brunt of storms coming from the south. Winds and waves gain force unimpeded through the Grand Bay and blow and crash upon the rocks beneath my cottage. Conversely, my cottage is protected from storms that come from the north or east by the hills behind. She faces west, which usually only brings mild weather.

As a boy, I spent every summer just two lots over with my grandmother and brother. My parents summer there now. I am grateful for the summers of my boyhood. They are happy remembrances: sun, swimming, boating, playing soldier with my cousin Bruce, fishing, exploring, and later when boyhood ended, the first exciting attempts of socializing with girls.

Bruce and I fished most days when we were young. We rowed out into the river in a rowboat, set anchor by a sunken wharf which was in front of my parents' cottage, and fished for perch. Occasionally we got an eel or a bass but we caught mostly the green-yellow, iridescent, scaly perch. We threw them back but kept count of our catch, adding up our totals throughout the summer. We discovered the best type of lure to catch perch was the curtain hangers from Bruce's cottage.

On sunny days it would be too hot to fish on the river, so we went to Buckley's Brook where it would be cool. We knew the best spot to dig worms, the best fishing holes, the best way to travel upstream, and where to stop before you came to bears! We traveled up the stream, hopping from fishing hole to fishing hole. We struggled through bush in some areas, jumped from rock to rock in others; always excited even though we had danced this dance many times before. No matter how hot the day, it was always cool down by the brook. We found the best fishing holes were created where the water was dark and foam formed on the surface from a small waterfall created by the brook falling over a natural dam. We never fought over who got what fishing hole; we would square it all up tomorrow. Nothing had to be said – friends are like that. We were in another world – a boy-world of filtered sun, coolness, boyish grins, laughs, and being friends.

Boys of ten would never talk of feelings or even know how to express such abstract ideas. As we grew, our interests diversified and the time we spent together became less and less, but when we are together today, the bond that formed when we were ten holds fast. We intuitively know who gets the next fishing hole; there is no contest between him and me. No need – boyhood friends are just like that.

We always made sure we were back home by noon because

the baker, milkman, or grocery man might show up on the hill, blowing his horn. There was a treat waiting for us: the grocery man had chocolate bars or candy; the baker, chocolate patty-pans; and even the milkman had those small containers of chocolate milk. These men probably never thought about the influence they had on our little lives, but even now, when we (my boyhood friends and I) get together, we often say, "Do you remember when the baker came, we stopped what we were doing and came running when we heard his horn? 'Baker! Baker!' We would all cry."

In later years, Jimmy Morrison, Steve Plummer, Bruce Barber, and I would swim, play tennis, boat, and at night we often loaded up our canoes and spent the night on deserted beaches. We took pride in our campfires, in building a 'lean-to' in case of rain, fixing and cooking our own grub, and talking adult. Important lessons on our road to independence, though we were just boys having fun.

As we grew older, the 'Point' became our foray into the graces of interacting with the opposite sex. 'Men of the campfire' turned into quivering idiots when confronted by these confusing yet mysteriously appealing playmates. A year ago they had been playmates, but this summer something happened – to them? – to us?

The first girl who ever paid attention to me was a girl from Toronto who was down visiting her cousin for two weeks. I don't know why she liked me, but I liked the attention. I was always the quiet one; I existed on the periphery in my circle of friends. I preferred it that way. But she saw me there and drew me out. Two weeks flew by and alas my first love had to leave. I was curious about what had happened – *why did a girl from Toronto find me appealing? The girls in my class at school had never given me any notice. I don't think they knew I existed. Maybe it was the new hair growth on my legs or maybe on my chest – two or three – or maybe it was those hormones I'd been reading about? Whatever, perhaps Linda or Pam or Barbie in my class will notice me this year!* Whatever Jane saw, Linda, Pam, and Barbie missed it; I was still invisible to them – the same ol' Shawn.

At the 'Point' I met my first long-term girlfriend – Debbi who became my high school sweetheart. We went out for over three years. We should have been dating other people, but even knowing that, I probably wouldn't have changed anything. High school sweethearts are special – so many new experiences, and those years can be so dynamic and exciting.

Buckley's Cove held many memories for me and I wanted my children to experience cottage life on the Peninsula. We stayed at my parents' cottage for a few summers but I grew restless for my own place

My cottage is built of cedar logs with three small bedrooms in the back and a great room that comprises our kitchen and family room. The deck is large with an over-hanging roof, and most days I can work on my deck, free of the sun or rain. I am close to the rocky cliff and about twenty feet from the river. As I write this story, I am on the deck with the waves rolling onto the rocks.

The cliffs are responsible for the constant sound of water movement I hear while I sit in my cottage. I roamed these rocks in my youth, stepping out onto the old wharf at low tide, marvelling at how lichen can survive on these rocks, and watching the developing mosquito larvae in the pools formed by the rocky crevices. Off shore, cormorants dive for fish; an occasional loon comes over from the marsh across the river, and osprey soar overhead looking for a meal.

On the rocks, I had often sat contemplating building my floating dock. There were many things to take into account; I wanted to build it so it could be broken apart, floated over to the beach, and then hauled up by two men at the end of the season, before the ice came. I also had to consider the tides (the St. John River empties into the Bay of Fundy, which has the highest tides in the world). Winds from the south whip up huge wave formations. The river's water level tends to get lower as the summer progresses. And how was I to secure the dock to shore? I spent time on the rocks watching the river and designing. When I finally built the dock and had it in place, I built a path from my cottage, down the rocky cliff, and onto my dock.

I grew up with the rocks, I played on the rocks, and now I would never walk on those rocks. I guess it symbolized a loss of many things to me: the walk along the footpath to Sand Point, into the forest, along a stream, on the beach – gone.

I'm back at the cottage now; ramps have been built, the bathroom altered, poles put in for me to hang onto, but essentially it's the same. The cormorants still dive, the loons still cry, and the osprey still soar; my dock is gone but the rocks still remain, as they always will. I am happy being close to them, hearing the waves break on their face, that's good enough for me – it will have to be.

*   *   *

As my left arm improved, the nurses encouraged me to use it by brushing my teeth, combing my hair, and shaving. It frustrated me and there were times I felt like giving up but something would happen to encourage me to keep going. The nurses gave me practical advice based upon their experience and I listened closely. They instructed me on the best underwear for men in a wheelchair to wear. (My habit was boxers but they don't work well in a wheelchair, if you have to be pulled back as often as I do.) But why are the flies so complicated in briefs? It's hard enough getting access standing up but try it in a wheelchair. It took me awhile to discover the brand having the easiest access. (That's my secret.)

I used a commode for the first time in September. My sitting balance had improved enough to allow me to sit on a commode with a lap belt. Simple changes like this can be surprisingly liberating.

My first shower – I was wrapped in a blanket, placed on a commode and wheeled down the corridor to the shower. I was used to a shower rather than a bath and it felt great, but the best thing was, no more swinging on the Hoyer Lift. I felt more in control even though I couldn't lift my arms to help with the showering. The nurses hosed me down and scrubbed me with soap and shampooed my hair. I was quite familiar with the whole procedure: I used to do the same with my dog.

Bedtime became an irritant to me. I was prepared for sleep starting at 9 P.M. because the nurses had to bath me, brush my teeth, clean my tracheotomy tube, and start my tube feedings. This all took time, so I was resigned to starting early, but now I was free of the trach and my tube feedings and felt I should be allowed to stay up later. I found myself hiding like a child from the nurses to avoid my bedtime. Many of my fellow patients felt like me and we plotted schemes to allow us to stay up later.

The nursing staff had to do this because they wanted all the work done before the night staff of two people came on at 11 P.M.. I realized this but I still hated being told when to go to bed at the age of forty-seven. It's part of institutionalized living; I had to live with it.

I wouldn't have minded if I could have read. I always read before sleep; it has been a habit since childhood. I always have loved books. I love the feel and the smell of books. I love being taken to another world by only words; it's like dreaming really except that you are fully awake and someone else – whom you don't even know – is directing the scene. I think it's interesting how a person writing, maybe fifty years ago, can direct that scene for me now.

I listened to talking books, which were fine but it wasn't the same. I watched TV but it didn't fill the void. I was lost when they put me to bed early – mostly, I watched ballgames as the sleeping pills took their effect.

One day I turned a newspaper page. It was difficult, frustrating if the paper didn't lie down straight, but I did it. Gradually turning the pages became easier, and eventually I could read a book in bed with a laptop table my cousin Lynne had given me. There were many frustrations: I lost my page many times; the book might fall from my bed; turning one page as opposed to many was difficult, but it was worth it. I was reading.

I read hardcover books – paperbacks were much too difficult with one hand. I can now use my right hand enough to hold a paperback open. At first I read stories by stroke survivors, especially by brainstem strokes survivors, but I also read fiction. One of the first books I read was probably symbolic: *Going Inside*, by Alan S. Kesselheim. It is a story about the experiences the author and his wife shared canoeing along a Canadian river up north and holding over for a winter. I thoroughly enjoyed it and being transported to a wilderness freedom I may never enjoy again.

I was reading; there was no need to hide from the nurses any longer.

I am lucky I enjoy reading, for as the saying goes, 'You can never be bored if you are a reader'. And you have time to read with this condition. And read. And read...

* * *

Locked in. I saw the irony of my having this condition now that I was slowly emerging from my cocoon. I had suffered from agoraphobia or an irrational fear of not having control over a situation from my twenties to mid-thirties. I felt a need to leave when I wanted, without causing a commotion, for example, in a plane, restaurant, line-up, driving as a passenger, or even a barber's chair. I feared vomiting or fainting in front of everyone, thereby bringing attention to myself. But if I drove the car, or if I sat in the end seat of an aisle, or perhaps if I controlled the plane, I would be fine. (However, the other passengers would require professional help.) It seems so foolish to me now but most phobias are.

It probably started as I commenced university but didn't become full-blown until I was in my early twenties. The first attack happened while I was eating supper at my girlfriend's home. Her family was large (eight siblings) and we were all around the dining table having a meal when I suddenly felt hot, then nauseated, followed by sweating and nervousness. I thought I was about to pass out. I never informed anyone; I just quietly stopped eating and hung on. I know now that it was a panic attack, but at the time I had no idea.

I made excuses, thinking I must be suffering from hypoglycemia, or ulcers, or later on, in my new but green medical wisdom; dumping syndrome. I denied the truth. I think I knew quite early what was wrong – *Shawnie boy – You are nuts!* – I couldn't accept it – I'm not alone, most people would rather have some pathology wrong with them than accept a mental problem.

The phobia advanced: in movie theatres, I had to be on an aisle seat; if I went to a restaurant, I had to be near the exit; line-ups bothered me; and air travel became a major anxiety. In some of these situations, the major anxiety occurred before I actually had the experience. Panic attacks are not pleasant and I became fearful of the fear. I eventually knew what they were but knowing doesn't help – they made me feel worse than anything I ever experienced from my stroke.

Probably the worst thing about a panic attack is that nothing does happen. You survive to have another, and no one has any idea what you just went through. My panic disorder went on for years and then it started happening in the office. In the morning and at noon my unconscious mind became aware that I was stuck there for hours – I couldn't get out without going past all my waiting patients. I was trapped – not in control. As silly as it sounds, I panicked before my office began, morning and noon. Again, once I was underway, I grew more relaxed.

Repeated exposure was not working; my phobia remained and did not lessen. I read books on the subject and even counselled patients with similar problems, often referring those same people to psychiatrists or psychologists. "Now, now," I'd say, when they acted dismayed at being referred to a shrink, "you are not crazy. The brain gets sick like any other organ – it gets sick differently – society has a poor attitude to mental illness. You shouldn't think of yourself as weak."

How hypocritical! I was keeping my dirty secret to myself; Jill was the only one who knew and I don't think I was completely honest with her as to the extent of my phobia. I needed to tell my own family doctor or refer myself to a psychiatrist or psychologist. I felt embarrassed with the thought of having a phobia over such silliness; it lowered my self-esteem. I chose to accept it and put up with it, but it made my life miserable.

Panic attacks are so devastating that it left me weak, quiet, a pitiful character really. I felt inferior for being unable to beat this thing. It was selfish of me not to seek help because I was less than I could have been for Jill. So I was stuck by being too proud to seek help. Foolish man! I, in effect, chose to make my life miserable. However a wonderful thing happened in my mid-thirties: I became depressed. I'm being sarcastic, because depression was anything but wonderful. It was like a big, black pit and you're never going to find your way out. It was cold and lonely in there. I could share the feelings of panic with Jill, but there is no way to share depression, nor would I want to. I was on my own, and this time I knew I couldn't live with it: I had to turn to someone for help.

It started out with a decrease in my appetite, especially in the morning – improving as the day wore on, so that by bedtime I was ravenous. Then my sleep became disturbed; I usually fell asleep fine, exhausted by the stress of the day, but within a few hours I awoke for a night of tossing and turning. I felt agitated the longer I lay awake, and by morning when I had to get up, I struggled, feeling anything but refreshed. My mood became depressed in the morning, improving by the evening. I felt my ability to concentrate at work slipping – my mind wandering as my patients told me of their symptoms. I lost weight and tiredness set in, a fatigue that left me legs trembling with any exertion.

Clinically, I was curious to be experiencing these symptoms. Depression was one of the most common illnesses I saw. A day as a family doctor did not go by without diagnosing a new case or following up a depressed patient. Now I was that patient.

Patients had not exaggerated the fatigue experienced in depression. I was amazed at how physically tired depression made me feel. I was confronted with these symptoms each day, and a part of me was fascinated to experience them. But the depressed mood state, the diurnal variation of the mood, the sleep disturbance, the appetite disturbance, and the lack of concentration were plain for me to see. I couldn't deny this: I was depressed.

There were probably a number of events that had happened that led to this depression. This is true for most depressions. Usually there is not one event you can pinpoint that leads to a depression. It does happen – sometimes grief over a lost loved one can go on too long and lead to an endogenous depression, but usually that type of depression is reactive and is best handled with supportive psychotherapy. A clinical or endogenous depression results from depletion or imbalance of neurotransmitters. My imbalance of neurotransmitters probably resulted from a number of situations. How life events and our reaction to them result in physical changes in the chemicals of our brain is unknown.

My underlying phobia no doubt played a major role in becoming ill – the old noggin had had enough. Also, at that time, I was under some financial strain because I and a group of physicians were developing a medical clinic; a number of my patients became ill from a flu shot administered at my office a few months before; and a patient not much older than I, whom I grew close to, expired with a form of hypoprothrombinemia.

Dave suffered from a type of phobia and I, of course, related to him. When he developed the blood problem (an inability of the bone marrow to produce platelets) we had no haematologist in Saint John. I sent him to Halifax for treatment, and after hospitalization down there lasting a few months, they sent him back to me. Things were going downhill and he continued to be my responsibility. I phoned the haematologist regularly, followed his directions but to no avail, Dave's platelet count (the blood cells we use for clotting) remained dangerously low. One night in his sleep he had a cerebral haemorrhage. I expected it but I had hoped a miracle would happen and one morning I would walk in and find the platelet count had risen. That's the damn thing about hypoprothrombinemia: occasionally that does happen and the bone marrow suddenly starts working.

Dave exasperated me because he kept a graph of his platelet count on the hospital room wall, plotting it every day and being encouraged by a small rise. I knew the rise was not significant and told him so, but I couldn't dash his hopes altogether. He never let me talk to him or his family about what could happen because he wanted no negativity. That's fine but I felt his family was ill prepared for what did occur. I found looking after Dave very stressful and with those added stresses I alluded to, a few months after Dave's death, I became depressed.

Jill couldn't believe I was depressed – a little down maybe – but not depressed. The psychiatrist likewise was surprised – I didn't seem depressed when he had seen me around, but when I explained to him my symptoms, he agreed: I was suffering from a depression.

I said the depression was a wonderful thing that happened to me, and it was. The depression finally prompted me to see someone and reveal that I suffered from a panic disorder. Just being able to tell somebody about my phobia was a relief, but also in taking my history he found reasons why I should be prone to developing this phobia. It was like someone turned on light in some dark tunnel in my brain – why hadn't I thought of this? Of course! This is cognitive therapy and it helped greatly in my recovery, but explaining why I suffered from this fear did not cure my problem – I wish it were that easy.

He prescribed an antidepressant drug that worked like a

charm on my depression, and as an added benefit, it also blocked my panic attacks. Within two weeks my depression was lifting and by four weeks it was nearly resolved. Treatment for depression often has to continue for six months, assuming there are no setbacks. Meanwhile my panic attacks were being blocked. I found I could go into restaurants and not worry – I enjoyed myself. I could sit in the middle of a row or go on planes without a worry. My brain soon learned that there was nothing to fear in these situations as the drugs blocked the anxiety.

Phobias are often caused by events or fears that start in our childhood.

With the drugs' help I took charge and thereby changed my life. So you see, the depression was a blessing and it caused another change in me. Prior to this I never gave psychotherapy much credit; I thought the only cure for mind disorders was drugs. After my experience I saw the value and need for this in my practice. I referred to psychotherapists earlier and more often than in the past. I started to delve into the past more with my patients who were suffering from neurosis. I started booking a long therapy session at the end of the day for patients I perceived as needing it. I grew to love this time; there is no time in a busy practice to fit in this type of session during the day, but as a last appointment for the day, it worked well.

I was amazed at the wealth of information I obtained, but whether it was worth the effort in view of the results is questionable. People enjoyed the ability and opportunity to talk; I think most of all they perceived that someone cared – or at least, I hoped they did.

Depression changed my life for the better; I loved living. I think it made me a better doctor, and I hope it showed me that something positive could come from a negative thing. I'm hoping and trying to make positive things happen from this stroke. I've enjoyed life to the fullest since my depression and I'm not stopping just because I've had a stroke.

So you see how ironic it was that I should be 'locked in'. If there was any situation that I was not in control of, it was being 'locked in'. Every body movement or function except for eye movement was in the control of someone else. Someone wiped my nose, my bum; they fed me, made me defecate; turned me in bed: I was dependent upon someone for every aspect of living. It was perhaps the agoraphobic's nightmare and I lived through it without a panic attack, without a whimper. It was like I had been prepared.

*   *   *

The Saint John Medical Society had that benefit dance in my honour. They made a video of the dance and get-well wishes from people attending. I was still emotionally labile and cried when shown the video by Dr. Mike Morse and Bill Tait, a drug detail representative who had helped organize the event. The generous words expressed to me touched my soul and made me cry. I felt like Tom Sawyer witnessing his own funeral.

I now had a bushel basket full of letters and cards from my patients. I had a hard time reading their generous words without crying. One of my patients, Chris Collrin, who taught Transcendental Meditation, offered to teach me the method. I had expressed interest while in practice but never found the time to do it. Chris taught my wife and me the method at home, and near the end of the sessions there is a ceremony. I laughed out loud while he carried out this supposedly solemn ceremony. I pinched myself to stop laughing; I tried thinking sombre thoughts; I tried to remove myself from this scene – nothing helped. It wasn't funny, but whenever I found anything the least bit happy, I broke into gales of laughter. Likewise anything the least bit sad, I cried. This emotional instability continued to plague and embarrass me.

I dared not go to a comedy or sad movie in a theatre. Pierre, the brain trauma victim whom I mistook as 'not right in the head', went to the same show, one night, as I did. Pierre had a funny sense of humour; he often had me laughing in the cafeteria, so when he started to laugh about something during a movie in a crowed theatre – that made me laugh just hearing him laugh, and soon the both of us were laughing, uncontrollably, about…? I knew in situations like this people thought I must be simple, but knowing this only made me laugh more.

I felt inadequate, incomplete as a human being by not having control of my emotions. It was as though someone else controlled my laughter or crying. While I laughed, I would pray, *Please God help me stop this – I do not find this funny.*

I hoped Transcendental Meditation would tranquilize my soul and maybe I would gain control over my emotions; I tried it but I kept falling asleep. It is supposed to be practiced before breakfast and supper. I couldn't ask the nurses to get me up but I asked them to awaken me, and when I tried to meditate in bed, I quickly fell asleep. In the afternoon I was so tired from my therapies that I fell asleep once again. If the object of TM was to relax me, I suppose it did work, but I couldn't really practice the discipline with drugs on board and in an institution. I expect it is a valuable tool for relaxing, increasing energy, and happiness; I was sorry I couldn't use it.

I could have used energy, inner peace or whatever it took, because on the ward I learned first hand what constipation felt like. All my life I went daily; I had never reason to think about it. I treated patients who complained of constipation, for it was a daily complaint in the hospital brought about by sudden inactivity. I must admit I thought the nurses were all anally fixated. Often the first thing they related to me in the morning was who 'went' and who didn't. I prescribed without giving much thought about what the patient must be going through.

Pay back! I found out why the bowel movement is the holy grail of hospitalized patients. It isn't fun being constipated – is it? I'm sorry I was so indifferent about it. I will spare you, the reader, with all the details, but suffice it to say, two years later the struggle continues, but what goes in has to come out. I'm testing that theory.

*   *   *

Speech lessons were tedious. Twice a day I tried to regain that which I had lost. It seemed to me a big part of 'who I am' left with my voice. That is not true, but at the time I mourned my loss. My voice still exists in its former intonation: on the telephone – "You have reached the home of Jill and Shawn Jennings, we are not at home – please leave a message after the beep. Thank you". And on a few tapes I had recorded myself singing and playing the guitar. But I'm still "me" regardless of what my voice sounds like.

It is not strange listening to my voice in the past; it does not make me melancholy – that was then and this is now. Two different things – look ahead – never live in the past.

I must have taxed Beth's patience for as she tried to get me to say 'moo', I broke into laughter. I felt so embarrassed by my apparent hilarity over her lessons; I apologized to her every time even though I knew she understood.

Actually it was quite sad; I had a hard time saying 'moo'. I would joke around and tell everyone, through my letter board, that Beth was trying to make me sound like a cow, but underneath that humour I was quite anxious. I did not have enough breath support to say a few words – such as they were. And my pronunciation was extremely poor. People had a hard time making out anything although I sounded understandable to my ear. I was shocked when Beth recorded me; it made me realize that I presented, to those who didn't know me, a far different person than who I was inside.

During speech lessons, Beth had me begin with a consonant and add all the vowels, for example: 'maa, mee, mii, moo, muu', or 'saa, see, sii, soo, suu.' Each word, each sound was a battle but it was only the beginning. Those sounds said using the middle of the tongue were easier, like 'm'; greater frustration came from trying to say soft sounds like the 'h' or sounds made with the anterior part of the mouth like 'v' or 'f' or the back of the tongue like 'k' or 'g'. I couldn't end words: 'whaa r ya doin' tani?' (What are you doing tonight? Said in a slur – words running together.).

I was more tired after speech than I ever was after physio or OT. The amount of energy I used to say simple phrases for a half hour far exceeded the results. Part of this energy was wasted, for a lot of the air came out my nose. My soft palate was paralysed, so it dangled down the back of my throat. When speaking, the palate is supposed to close, sealing the nasal passages and thereby allowing all the air volume to come out your mouth and be used for speech. A good portion of my air (and that wasn't a big amount to begin with) came out my nose, leaving only a small amount to use for speech. My muscles of respiration were paralysed; the muscles required to move my vocal cords were spastic; it all seemed too much at times but Beth always encouraged me and small gains were being made. I kept plugging on and I still do. I do stomach crunches; I work on word inflection in a sentence; I breath into a spirometer daily for more breath support – nothing comes spontaneously; nothing comes quickly without effort, but it does improve for some brainstem stroke victims. I'm so fortunate to be getting some function back; I don't forget that and I try harder tomorrow.

*   *   *

Try harder – tricky for us with rigidity and tone. The harder I tried to do something like bend my hip, the higher the tone in the muscle became and the harder it was to bend my hip. I use tone to my advantage sometimes as in standing, but don't ask me to move from that spot.

Mereille *did* ask me to move from that spot. I had been standing with a table in front of me while I put weight on my hands – this was to reduce tone in my legs and arms. Doreen always came to work with Mereille, and together they had been addressing my posture (sitting and standing) and balance. I couldn't perform the acts of sit-to-stand or stand-to-sit, rolling over or lie-to-sit; I was stiff, my pelvis and back were all one. "Bend at the waist, Shawn! Bend those hips!" they cried. My muscles, because of the tone, would not let go.

Standing is a good way to relieve tone so Doreen and Mereille had me do this often throughout the sessions, but the day came when they asked for more – stepping. I was excited; this was what I wanted to do – now we were cooking!

Excitement soon turned to frustration as my legs showed no desire to move. They moved them for me. Mereille steadied me from the back, correcting my posture, gait, and pelvic movement; Doreen steadied my walker and hand control, while Betty or Jill moved my feet. My entourage and I must have been a curious sight as we moved down the gym.

I realized if I was to walk it wouldn't happen today or tomorrow, but I grew disappointed at my lack of progress. Mereille and Doreen didn't stop however; they faithfully took me on a walk daily. Despite telling me I would not walk normally, they hadn't given up. This gave me hope for some type of walking.

It was hard to watch others progress. Stroke survivors started walking. These stroke victims were always the one-sided type, or cerebral; I had no other brainstem stroke survivors to relate to, so I watched them. I was happy for them as they progressed from immobility to walker with assistance, to walker alone, to quad canes, to cane, to finally walking alone. I was well aware that I was different and that I couldn't compare my stroke to their type of stroke, but I couldn't help it.

I *was* happy for their improvement but there was a part of me that cried, '*Why? Oh why can't that be me? – Just one step– just some improvement that I could see.*'

I was envious; I wanted a 'eureka'. I couldn't believe how

calm everyone was accepting their improvement as though it was a natural course of events. They worked hard for what they got and I suppose to them it seemed slow, but I felt that I worked hard too and I deserved some reward.

I was unique around there but I started to feel more akin to the quadriplegics. I suppose it is natural that we tend to seek out members in our society who are similar to ourselves. After all, I was quadriplegic also, only from a stroke not trauma. I shared some of the same problems as they did, and the quads in my Rehab could do some tasks better than I and some not as well.

There was a big difference: I had a chance to improve over a few years; they could only improve to a point and then they would have to await a medical breakthrough. I realized I had little to complain about as I watched Amanda and Todd struggle.

*   *   *

Amanda arrived at Stan Cassidy during the summer. She was in her early twenties and a young mother. Her daughter, Mackenzie, was about one year old and quickly became the darling of Stan Cassidy. Amanda had broken her neck in an all-terrain vehicle accident. She drove the ATV up a hill to her car as she left a party; she wasn't going far but during that simple ride the ATV flipped, changing her life forever. A simple mistake can take a life, or change a life, or sometimes does nothing but cause a chuckle. Amanda's passenger was not hurt but she was left quadriplegic for life.

Amanda had bright eyes and a cheery disposition despite her circumstances. It was impossible not to like her; she did not hide her emotions and took no care to pretend around others for the sake of propriety. She tried to control her life and this resulted in frustrations, anger outbursts, and more than once, phone-slams. Yet Amanda was tender and giving in spirit. I couldn't smile, talk, or gesture in any manner to make conversation, yet she always included me in her conversations, "Isn't that right, Shawn? What do you think, Shawn?"

She was a buzz saw of activity and emotions undoubtedly resulting from her drugs and circumstance, but underneath I suspect she was probably quite a bubbly young lady before her accident. She flew around Stan Cassidy in her power chair in one speed – fast. She twirled around in circles and the chair became an extension of her persona. As she watched TV she moved her wheelchair, turning one way or another, always on the move, as though the chair was a part of her hyperactivity. This was a young girl with things to do, adventures to experience, and loves to explore.

My heart went out to her. She will never know the influence she had on my emotional recovery. How could I feel sorry for myself when Amanda faced far worse prospects of recovery than I did? Oh, Amanda wasn't brave, nor did she even try to be stoic, but Amanda was real. She did not try to hide behind some romantic ideal of how a heroic quadriplegic should act: she would laugh at that. No, Amanda lived in the present tense; it wasn't pretty, it wasn't fun, there was not a damn thing romantic about it, but it was her reality.

Maybe Amanda was a big crybaby when interacting with her doctor and nurses, or maybe Amanda was a big, brave girl all the time – I don't know. But I do know Amanda was real and I thank her for being her.

Todd became my friend, roommate, and in a way an inspiration also. Todd became quadriplegic in a motor vehicle accident. Late one night he drove home from some event. He wasn't drinking but he was tired. That would be his mistake, for he fell asleep, and when he woke up he was lying in a ditch unable to move. He was quadriplegic for life (hopefully not, maybe a medical breakthrough will happen) starting in his early twenties.

Todd had already been there a few months when I arrived. He had red hair and a round, cheerful face; I imagined him as a child – energetic, impish, an 'I never took to schoolin' type of guy, a regular Huck Finn. He reinforced my impressions from the stories he told me. He talked of adventures that happened in his youth, life in rural New Brunswick, in small towns, his loves. Rural life trivia: "Ever eat squirrel? Not bad. I wouldn't eat skunk though."

Todd never talked a lot but he was the first to talk to me for any length of time. He made no assumptions of my abilities; he spoke to me as an equal. Most impressive of all his qualities: he always tried to understand me despite my dysarthria (speech impediment). He never said, "Oh, is that so," as people were apt to do when they couldn't be bothered trying or were too tired to decipher my speech. I understood people getting frustrated; *I* got frustrated trying to be understood, but Todd never appeared to. He and Jill comprehended my speech better than even I; *how did he (or she) get that? I didn't even understand what I said.*

Todd and I laughed. We laughed about situations we got into, our conditions, stories we shared, jokes, and typical dumb, male humour.

Todd loved country music and always had the country channel on TV. I liked rock, folk, jazz, new age, almost any type, with country music being on the low end of the scale. We had many good-natured laughs over this and he showed me the value of this music form (not to mention the pretty girls in country music!). I told him he was sent to torture me with his brand of music. Don't tell my friends, etc...

Todd was human, and although he put up a brave front, especially during the day, I often heard him struggle with emotions at night. He fought with the bed sheets, trying to turn; his remote might fall just beyond his grasp; his bladder might spontaneously empty; the pain that came in his body might be tormenting him; and besides the physical distress, I couldn't imagine the emotional turmoil that my friend must be going through.

I had been able to find true love – Jill. I had raised and had the thrill of raising children. I had felt the joy of coming home from work and having kids rush to me with unconditional love. I had had a productive and self-fulfilling work life. Although these things were still obtainable for my friend, I knew it would be a struggle for him. I didn't know if he knew that – that life still goes on for the disabled. I thought he might be thinking that life had stopped; that he would never find a job, hunt again, or find someone to love.

I heard him cry softly during the nights, sometimes. It might have been with pain, frustration, or emotional turmoil; I never questioned him. I think he would have been uncomfortable discussing emotions; so as the day dawned, we moved on, and forgot our demons of the night.

Todd struggled hard to do things on his own; he became as independent as he could and in doing so he gained my admiration. Like Amanda, he demonstrated to me how fortunate I was; I couldn't feel sorry for myself while these two young people were struggling bravely for some form of independence. I thank Todd for becoming my friend, and although he didn't intend it, he became instrumental in my emotional recovery.

CHAPTER 10 – OCTOBER

I didn't require as much care now that my feeding tube and trach were gone, and that meant I didn't warrant a private room. My first roommate was ideal for my transition. His name was Colin, about my age, friendly, but quiet. He had suffered the rupture of a brain aneurysm. His body had responded quite well: he was walking, using one arm and talking well. However his thinking process was disordered and he had expressive aphasia (he couldn't find the right words to express his thoughts). We were quite the pair – he couldn't explain himself without getting mixed up and I couldn't physically say what I wanted. We did communicate somehow but mostly we just shook our heads and laughed at our failings.

Colin lived in Fredericton so he went home a lot, often leaving me with the room to myself. It was similar to my previous room, the walls of cement brick painted white, a large wall of windows, a closet, and bathroom. The only difference was, there were now two beds instead of one. I shared the small, ancient bathroom with the adjacent room containing two more people. My window looked out onto a small parking lot, seldom used as it was at the back of the building. A basketball net (used even less) sat silently in the yard awaiting a patient to explore his or her capabilities. Stan Cassidy's inadequacies as a major rehabilitation centre for New Brunswick became more apparent to me.

How dare they treat people with life-changing disabilities this way. I must admit I never thought much about rehabilitation when I actively worked. Rehabilitative medicine has always been the poor sister in medical funding, but I felt there was no excuse in providing disabled people with a facility that had inadequately sized rooms. Disabled people have always had to fight for their rights – access to all public places is still an ongoing battle – cut away curbs, public transportation, parking places for *truly* disabled people, etc. It looks like this is a similar situation. It looks like the government will continue giving lip service to disabled people unless we bring the issue to the forefront.

I was quite comfortable here and I didn't hate Stan Cassidy. The staff made the difference, but I wished they had a better facility to work in, to enable them to better serve the disabled.

By this month – October – my sliding board was gone forever. I pivoted from my bed to chair with help, using a walker. I could not stand up or sit independently, but I was happy without my board.

At physiotherapy they started to use a 'Lite Gait', which was a treadmill upon which I was suspended from above by straps that were tied around my waist and groin. It was supposed to signal my brain as to the normal pattern of walking while taking away gravity. The signals weren't getting through; I continued with high tone in my legs, making it hard for me to bend my knees and flex my hips. In fact the Lite Gait made the tone worse – I needed gravity – weight on my feet to reduce the tone.

Doreen tried everything to facilitate my sit to stand but I couldn't break the tone in my back. Rolling myself over in bed became a goal and we tried repeatedly, but I couldn't break the tone to flex my hips, turn my shoulders, and follow with my pelvis.

Tone continued to plague me even in my speech. My facial muscles were tight, and even if I did manage to break the tone and move my lips, my laryngeal muscles were often tight and my voice came out like a squeak.

I shaved (lots of razor burn) and brushed my teeth (toothpaste down my arm, on my pants) and after a lot of effort, my left arm and hand were improving but my right arm and hand remained paralysed. Up until this time I hoped my right arm was just months behind my left arm but that looked more and more unlikely. The left arm had progressed from arm control of my wheelchair to hand control. I could now go where I wanted in the wheelchair with no effort. I thought that maybe by transferring the hand controls to the right side, it would force my right hand to work. Doreen agreed to let me try. I tried – it was very frustrating – but I never succeeded. My hand continued to flex into a claw, unable to open, a useless thing really. I had to use my left hand to open my right hand up and place it on the joystick. I was unable to externally rotate my arm (turn outwards) and tried to resist the temptation of using my left arm to aid the right. But sometimes you have to get there, you know? (After my stay at Stan Cassidy, effective therapeutic evidence for constraint therapy came out. This entails restraining your good arm, thereby forcing you to use the affected arm. I would wager that tone was too strong in my arm for that technique to be effective, but I would have tried.) After months of trying, I gave up and Doreen put my controls back to my left side.

* * *

I continued to go home every weekend and this made staying at Stan Cassidy bearable; it gave me something to look forward to. I went home on Friday afternoon and returned Monday morning, thereby only spending four nights at the Centre. Jill was the reason I was able to do this; I was a heavy care, I needed assistance to stand, sit, lie, roll, and eat. The insurance company continued to pay for a nursing assistant at night.

It is a shame that insurance companies make life harder for the disabled. They always request documentation from professionals *at your expense* and hold up payment or authorization until they receive it. The disabled, especially a newly disabled person, is having a hard enough time dealing with their life-change without having to worry about money and care. It is a cruel endeavour and so unnecessary. I understand that insurance companies are subject to many cases of fraud, but assuming every case may be fraudulent is wrong. I know that, by being vigilant for fraud, the insurance companies are keeping our premiums lower…or are they keeping their profits higher?

In my case, I was quadriplegic. It would only take someone who represented the insurance company to come and see me. Then they would see that I couldn't stand, I couldn't use my arms; my wife couldn't possibly look after me 24 hours a day. Assume the client, especially one with a major illness, is telling the truth. If they won't see for themselves, don't wait for letters from the OT, physiotherapist, physician, and whoever else and stop payment until all documents are received! I am fortunate to have enough resources to be able to withstand these lulls but others may not be so lucky.

I saw many cases of this while working as a family physician. There were a few cases of client abuse (and I tried to point them out) but there were many more cases of abuse generated by the insurance companies. People pay high premiums for many years, and when tragedy does strike, the insurance companies should show more compassion than what they are exhibiting at present.

My disability insurance company has been fine; they have caused no problem at all. But my health insurance company has been stubborn. This type of treatment did not surprise me at all; I indicated to Jill to comply to their requests, no matter how silly it might seem, and not to take it personally. But Jill had not been conditioned to this type of treatment and found the obtaining of requested documentation stressful, tiring, and frustrating. The caregiver, already burdened by maybe a new role in the relationship, new responsibilities and tasks, is now asked to be responsible for the compiling of information…and it better be timely and correct or we won't pay you! Give the caregiver a break, insurance companies; if you want information, get it yourself!

At this point we were receiving no major obstacles from the insurance companies and renovations to my home were on schedule. The little talk I received from Doreen and Mereille worked and I had accepted that my life was never going to be the same. I was not going to walk upstairs to my bathroom, so if I was going to stay home, I had better make my downstairs completely accessible. The nagging concern about cost continued in the back of my mind but it had to be done. (Eventually my car insurance paid for the renovations). Jill handled the details of what to buy – type of shower, toilet, knocked out vanity, etc. – and I watched her in awe. Despite all this stress, she managed all details capably, and my admiration and love for her grew – if that was possible.

I felt hunger for the first time since my stroke. I was eating without supplementation, now that my 'milkshakes' were through. I wanted a thick, juicy steak but I didn't have the ability to chew. I had to be content with pureed – *patience, time* – I was happy just eating and hunger felt good, it was something normal.

At home the computer enabled me to contact the outside world. I continued to speak to friends via e-mail, visit disability sites, and exchange ideas with stroke survivors. My left arm improved enough to remove the armrest and use the mouse instead of the keyboard cursor, and I no longer needed a key guard.

I still felt restless in my wheelchair at times and had a need to get out onto a chair. However these feelings of restlessness were fading; I became more accustomed to my seat. The feeling of being restricted melted as I accepted the facts – *You are effectively a paraplegic, buckaroo! Oh maybe you'll fool them and walk – DON'T GIVE UP! – But here and now – you're in a wheelchair.* A few months ago I thought there was no way I'd get used to a wheelchair. But you do. You have no option.

* * *

In Fredericton I went to my first movie; in Saint John I went to my first hockey game. Patti, my nursing friend who had done so much for us, accompanied us. I enjoy watching hockey, the speed, the flow of the game, play patterns forming, defensive strategy, and the charged atmosphere in a close game. I grew up with hockey played on our backyard rinks and on the street.

We didn't play organized hockey – I don't know why? (Maybe Schoolboy Leagues but not Minor.) But my friends and I played a lot. I had frozen toes, like most Canadian boys, more than I care to remember as the recollection of the thawing process comes to mind. We never became real good hockey players, probably because we had no instruction, but we didn't care; amongst ourselves we had great games. We were Jean Belliveau, Bobby Hull, Norm Ullman, Alex Delvecchio, Dave Keon, or Gordie Howe. The sounds and exhilaration of the game never left me: skates crunching on ice, the chase for the puck, the perfect pass to someone in flight, and of course, picking the upper left corner of the net and the darn puck actually going there – the perfect goal. And when you go to bed that night, you see that goal again and again in your mind.

I was never good as a player, probably because I had no natural talent (I won't admit that to my kids) but I loved the game. I gave up playing around the time I entered high school. I was thin, and the only way to survive on the ice if you have no bulk is to be fast. I wasn't that either. I got banged around quite a bit one night, so I gave up the game, but not my enthusiasm.

I was thrilled to be back in the rink watching the Saint John Flames, a minor professional team. Four months ago I could barely raise my thumb. I had watched the Stanley Cup playoffs without interest, and now I was back in Harbour Station, the arena in Saint John. Many friends and patients came to greet me and wish me well. They were happy to see me, but no one was happier than I.

* * *

Life is often reflected in the games we play, but maybe sometimes the games we play reflect or possibly predict our lives.

When I was a child, my friends Allan and Ronnie and I would

watch "Western Theatre" on Saturday afternoon. CBC was the only channel we could obtain, so we didn't have much choice. Black and white thrillers of cowboys, Indians, rustlers, and no-good, gosh-darn varmints. It fed our eager imaginations, and soon after the show we would meet behind Al's house to act out our own tale.

Al's father owned a black car trailer that doubled as our stagecoach. We had six guns with leather holsters strapped to our legs by a piece of rawhide. My guns had silver barrels with western designs etched along their length. The handles were white with a horse head embossed on the sides. The handles were actually plastic but I imagined they were carved ivory. (I had no idea what ivory actually was but I heard a cowboy remark to another cowboy once about his gun being carved from pure ivory and they seemed to be impressed.) We could use blast cap strips – if we had them – and that was "way cool", but unnecessary for the plot; a 'bang-bang' did nicely, and besides we loved making the ricochet sound.

Al usually set the scene and we added suggestions. In fact we often got so carried away with the suggestions, we'd forget the premise and have to start all over again.

We often rode the stagecoach into Dodge with gold or a lovely young lady, the daughter of the General, when no-good bandits would come out of the woods to steal our precious cargo.

"There's one, Al! To your left." He fired and the varmint fell from his horse.

"One's hopped onto the stagecoach!" Ron struggled with him in hand-to-hand combat, nearly falling out a couple of times but each time managing to force his way back up. Suddenly I'm in trouble. An hombre has managed to climb onto the stagecoach behind me while Ron was grappling with his varmint, and he has me by the throat. I fight, but he has me good.

"Al!" I yell, motioning that I'm being strangled.

Al is driving the stagecoach but he does an incredible feat: he manages to wrap the driving reins around one leg, stand up, turn around, and slug my assailant over the head with his gun. (No wonder we love this guy as our director.)

"Thanks, partner."

Al shrugs it off like it was another day's work – no big deal.

Meanwhile, Ron has got rid of his bad dude by flipping him over his back onto a stump that was sticking up as our stagecoach drove by. (We never saw this in a cowboy movie but on a trading card. There was a series depicting the Civil War that was popular at the time, and it showed someone – maybe Stonewall Jackson – being thrown off his horse and impaled on wooden spears that had been driven into the ground for this purpose. Way too cool! We thought this was so cool we couldn't pass up the opportunity of incorporating this scene into our play. A bad dude always got impaled somehow along the way.)

We continued shooting until invariably Ronnie got shot. He went down with great fanfare, clutching his chest, grunting; then over the side he went with a fantastic tumble routine. (I suspect Ronnie got shot first because he would rather be playing cars. Cars were his passion, and continued to be his passion throughout life.)

This was the clue for my eventual demise. However I was not so eager to end our little play, and besides, I liked to play the struggling hero who gets shot and tells his pal to leave him.

"I'm shot, Al!" I grab my chest and fall to my knees. Al glances back. We have outdistanced the bandits – they have fallen on Ron and are taking his boots (I know, a feeble, unlikely plot but boots seemed valuable to cowboys; they were always trying on dead men's boots – and they always fit – and besides, we were only six years old).

We had time, so Al lifts me down from the stagecoach and cradles me on the ground.

"Hurt bad, partner?"

"Rec'in I'm not going to make it, Al."

"Hush now. We goin' get you a doc' and get you all fixed up

like, once we gets you into town."

"No Al, I've had the biscuit – (big cough here; blood comes up) – But you got to do me a favour. Leave me here."

"No way! I'll…"

"Listen to me, dagnabit! I can't go on – I'm goin' to die – But Al, listen to me – (I grab his shirt and bring him towards me. My words are becoming shallower and I pant between each word) – Ya' got to save the pretty miss from those bandits."

"I'm not abandoning you. You're like a brother to me." (Ronnie's getting a tad fed up by this point and he ruins our scene by saying, "Come on, guys!").

"Shut up!" we both yell.

"Ya' got to do me this one favour – give me a gun and I'll hold them off."

"No!"

"I want to die fighting. You wouldn't deny a dying man his last request – would you, Al?"

Al pulls out his gun and gives it to me. He climbs up onto the stagecoach, and with a 'Giddy up!' he drives away.

I lie waiting, and as the bandits come I kill a few, until they pump a few more bullets into me and I die. I can hear the music getting louder as the camera pulls away from the scene.

Al seemed to always get the girl, but no matter, I got to play the hero and Ronnie got off early to play cars. We played many variations of this, but Ronnie always seemed willing to get 'knocked off' early, and I loved being disabled by bullets. Often I was shot up bad but managed to make it back to town, staggering, and falling in a heap as the townspeople rushed to my side.

Years later Ronnie died in a snowmobile accident. He was in his early forties. At the age of forty-six, I had my stroke and became disabled. Al's had a tough life; he's had to dodge a lot of bullets but he's still riding.

I'm going to play the other scene, Al: I'm getting to

Dodge – shot up – but staggering in.

*   *   *

I guess my sex life has been healthy or whatever 'healthy' means in that connotation. Oh, I know, healthy means doing whatever, as long as both partners are comfortable with it. But 'healthy' does sound rather odd when used to describe sex, doesn't it? It isn't like a healthy habit we try to adopt, such as eating green vegetables to prevent cancer, or the cessation of smoking, or cutting down on fats, or getting exercise (well maybe sex could be considered an exercise!). I've never heard anyone prescribing sex twice a week for your health (although I can think of some who could benefit).

I understandably never thought about sex once from May to October. I don't remember a dream, thought, or fantasy of any type. I was now into my fifth month and I had not experienced an erection; not even an early morning erection signalling pee time! Since this was the area of my anatomy the nurses often tackled first to wash, I was always afraid they might find 'Henry' rising up to say 'hello' (friendly fellow but sometimes quite inappropriate). Thankfully it never happened but I grew curious with his non-appearance. I knew strokes had no bearing on the ability to have an erection – which proves it doesn't take brains... oh, never mind. It is not a recorded side effect of the drug I was taking. Maybe psychological, but why not the early morning erection?

A mild sexual dysfunction is common after a stroke – premature ejaculation, erectile dysfunction, performance anxiety, fear of causing another stroke, a myriad of problems. I knew all this and I knew I should have no reason for erectile dysfunction. I was more academically interested as to the cause; I was not really worried until...

Samantha (fictional name) was a pretty young nurse who always appeared cheerful, confident, and friendly, although she later admitted to me she had been rather wary of me because I was a doctor.

One night Samantha showered me. Usually the nursing assistants did this task, but for some reason that escapes me now, Samantha attempted the chore. After I showered, she wheeled me back to my bathroom to dry off. As she dried my feet a peculiar sensation came over me: I thought I was about to urinate. In a panic I started to warn Samantha, when I ejaculated onto my thigh. Luckily I had a towel covering my genitals. I had had no warning, no erection – nothing! My body went through powerful spasms of orgasm; my bottom slid out of the chair; my feet flew up in the air and I groaned.

"What was that?" Samantha said.

"Spa-spa-spa-spasm" I tried to say.

"I never saw you get spasms like that."

"Twi-twi-twi-twice a week."

"Are you OK?"

"I'll be fi-fi-fi-fine."

Samantha went back to drying my feet while I panicked. A smell pervaded our small room; at first I didn't recognize it but soon I remembered.

Oh no! Does she know what happened? Should I tell her?

I think Samantha had an idea because she slowly rose up; I was about to say something (or was I?) when Bessie (fictional name) walked in.

Bessie was an older nurse, matronly, I thought: *Oh Lord, how does this look? A middle aged old goat with a pretty young nurse, and the smell of sex in the air!*

There *is* no God because I wouldn't be alive right now. I thought dying was the only way out of this. Usually when confronted with a personal dilemma or crisis like this, I did what I always did – nothing. I froze. My mind went catatonic. Vapours of burnt wires drifted up from my head. Overload! Overload!

There are some things a man can explain, but sitting in a room with a pretty, young nurse with ejaculate on your thigh isn't one of them.

This was one of those no win situations like your wife asking you if she looks overweight. I was dead, dead, dead.

Bessie took over my care and prepared me for bed. She was about to take away the towel that was covering my genitals! I quickly pretended I was itchy and rubbed my thigh with the towel. I then let it fall to the floor and prayed I had been successful in removing the evidence. *Yes!*

While Bessie put me in my pyjamas, I noticed Samantha picking up the towel and taking it away. *Was she holding it different? Out to her side? Did she know? My imagination?*

I couldn't get to sleep; I fought the sleeping medication; my embarrassment over what had just occurred tormented me. And what had just occurred? I was not fantasizing about Samantha; Samantha had not done anything improper; I wasn't even thinking about girls or sex. Granted this probably wouldn't have occurred with Denis or Nadir, two male nurses – or at least I hope it wouldn't have happened or I would have been even more embarrassed! I don't have a foot fetish that I am aware of. What happened?

Another episode of spontaneous ejaculation without an erection happened a short time after. On this occasion the nurse was simply rubbing my sore shoulder and then suddenly, without warning – I ejaculate! Again completely asexual – my wife and two of my children were in the room. Talk about your wires being crossed!

It seemed I was super-sensitive to any stimulation. But don't be afraid to give me a hug if you see me, I won't ejaculate! It has never happened again.

I saw the humour in the whole scenario after I got over the acute embarrassment. *My friends will enjoy this story,* I thought. Then there came sadness after the humour. I still hadn't had an erection and this experience only heightened my anxiety. I loved Jill so much and it made me sad to think my sex life was over at the age of forty-seven.

Why do I even mention this episode? At risk of embarrassing myself, I want to point out that I, a doctor, who supposedly should know better, was anxious about my sex life after a stroke. It is very common for stroke survivors to be anxious about their sex life. It is often the unspoken fear of the patient, so it is imperative that a doctor or nurse bring up the subject, even if the patient seems reluctant. This is especially true for the brainstem stroke survivor who usually has more neurological deficits.

I used Debbie, a young nurse, who seemed willing to talk about sexual problems. She was easy to talk to, had a sunny personality, and was romantically involved with a paraplegic. Mostly we joked, but all the while she was making sure Jill and I knew sexual relationships still continue after a stroke. But I couldn't talk to her or anyone about my erection problem – I felt too embarrassed.

I told Jill what had happened when she came in the next day. I was not apprehensive to tell her; I was confident in our love and I knew she would take it as she did: she laughed. I told her about my anxiety about making love; it was the first time I brought up the subject.

I sometimes went down to Jill's apartment in the evening to break the monotony. We took the 'Handi-Bus' or, on a nice evening, she wheeled me down. About two weeks after my embarrassing episode with Samantha, in the apartment, Jill and I made love. We both cried after. I cried because I loved her so; I cried because she was so familiar; I cried because this love making was so unfamiliar; I cried because my arms were useless, I couldn't hold her, caress her; I cried because I was happy being back with her again.

* * *

Colin became a day patient – living at home and presenting

daily for therapy. Rather than give me a new roommate, they switched people to different rooms and I ended up in a ward. The ward was long and narrow consisting of four beds arranged side by side like an army barracks except I think with less room. I resided at the end of the row against the wall.

There were only two other patients besides me in the ward during my stay there. We all had suffered strokes and I, at the age of 47, was the oldest. Strokes are usually thought of as being a disease of the elderly; our room proved that impression wrong. Strokes are certainly more common in the elderly but they do happen in younger people.

Duane was in his late twenties. He had been involved in a motor vehicle accident, suffering some broken bones and contusions but nothing life-threatening. A few months after the accident he suffered a cerebral stroke. He had regained walking and speaking ability but worked on strengthening his gait and improving his affected arm.

Jim was in his late thirties and he had suffered a cerebral stroke also. He had all the major chemical and genetic risk factors for stroke; but he didn't have the body habit of a person who would have a stroke (neither did Duane), he was not overweight and was very active. Jim walked and talked well also and worked on the same goals as Duane.

They were both excellent fellows, respecting each other's personal space, quiet when need be, but we shared the need to laugh. Duane was thoughtful and quiet – I think he missed his wife and baby a lot. Kevin was more talkative; he bedded beside me and was a great help to me. He loved the Boston Red Sox, so he and I often watched the ball games on TV while we fell asleep.

Being on a ward did not change the nursing routine: up at 7:15 A.M., breakfast at 8, therapy starting at 9, lunch at 12, therapy resuming at 1 P.M., therapy finished around 3 or 4, supper at 4:45, to bed by 10 (if they could find us).

One day I got a break from that routine by having a student nurse assigned to me. She was very pleasant and I enjoyed the company as she stayed by my side throughout the day. I'm afraid I may have caused her some distress, because after a few days she had to ask me a series of questions. One of the questions was pertaining to what I missed most about being there. The answer was easy but I burst out crying, "My kids!"

Most of the time I tried not to think of them: Colin being so responsible and kind, looking after his younger sisters; Beth – cooking the meals and doing well in Grade 12 – an exciting yet important time of her life – and I wasn't there to help her; and Tara, in Grade 8, continuing her excellence in school and activity in sports, with little guidance from us. They could give me no greater gift then demonstrating to me that we raised them to be responsible and independent.

Still, I cried as I said goodbye to them after each weekend: I missed the idle chatter over meals, the laughter, and the bond of a family together. I hated thinking of them arising each morning on their own, making breakfast, going to school; they had ample opportunity to skip school but they never did. They could have not studied in the evenings but their marks showed they did. I was so proud of them but I missed them so; I let my emotions go in front of this student nurse who must have felt terrible at causing me pain. I thought I was getting control of my emotions but the tears would not stop, no matter how hard I willed them to cease.

I grew tired of my disobedient emotions; I grew tired of the nursing routine; I grew tired of Stan Cassidy. I knew I had to stay to improve so I never seriously considered quitting but I started to get an inkling that progress was slowing down. November – December would prove to be a major turning point in my life.

CHAPTER 11 – NOVEMBER – DECEMBER

Mereille tried to induce functional responses in my legs by using different exercises. I walked on stairs, treadmills, with splints, without splints. I had electric myographic stimulation to my muscles. I visualized myself walking: *nice and easy, Shawn. It's a nice day and I'm walking on a beach. My legs are relaxed.* The results were always the same: my tone did not allow my muscles to relax.

Mereille always remained optimistic and encouraged me but I could feel the change in my body. Up to then my body either obtained spontaneous return of movements or with hard work, function improved. I was spinning my wheels. I noticed I wasn't getting the same results, no matter how hard I worked.

Up to now I had felt like my body was thawing out. Each day a new part of my body worked better than the day or week before. Then I could feel the change – my body seemed to stop – it seemed that was it – no more improvement.

The implications were devastating: *I had hope. I had crawled out of being 'locked in'. I was standing with a walker. I was using my left arm to eat, brush my teeth; I couldn't stop there! Don't leave me with the walker in my hand. Please, don't be that cruel. Please!*

I couldn't help but implore God not to let my progress stop here, but to give me the strength and spirit to continue. I didn't want to think negatively but it got harder not to; I thought that the window for improvement had closed. It had been six months, so maybe I'd have to accept it. Was this the plateau they talked about?

Again the old problem of when to accept and when to keep fighting but I realized: *If I give up, I will never improve. Never. Never. Never. That is a certainty. But if I keep trying and try not to be discouraged, I have a chance. I'll keep praying for strength to continue on – but I'll do it! – I will walk someday – if God will help me not get discouraged, I will do the rest!*

So I came to believe that my rate of progress had slowed down but had not finished. It was discouraging to think that my rapid improvement phase had ended and this was as far as I had advanced; it was a disappointment but not the end of my journey out of the tunnel.

I didn't want to give in, and with my new attitude I wanted to go the extra mile – I wanted to fight – never give in! I balked when Doreen approached me about ordering my own power chair; I did not want to surrender the possibility of never wheeling my own chair. I thought if I was forced to use my right arm to wheel my own wheelchair, it would improve.

The tone in my right hand prevented me from opening my grip, so once my hand was on the wheel, it wouldn't let go. My chest muscles wanted to pull my arm into my chest; they didn't like to relax and let my arm extend outward to the wheel.

I think Doreen knew I was wrong, but to her credit she saw I was adamant and helped me choose a manual chair. When it arrived a few weeks later, I was determined to use only this chair from now on. I pivoted in and tried to wheel down the corridor. I went maybe a foot. My right hand refused to let go, and in the end Doreen wheeled me back to my room before lunch.

I tried to use my manual chair and forsake the power chair, but I wasn't making it to my therapies; someone always had to come and rescue me. So I gave up trying the manual throughout the day and went back to my power chair. But in the evening Jill helped me practice up and down the corridor. My right hand grip never eased up, my skin chaffed, and blisters formed on my thumb. Night after night we practiced but the tone never relented. I was wrong – I found out that you don't always get rewarded for effort; sometimes the physical limitation is too great. That is the hard truth, but as in life, if you hit a wall, back up and go another way.

I did no better with my speech. My palate continued to be stubborn and did not close when I tried to speak. My facial muscles and tongue wouldn't cooperate and my breath support was minimal. I wasn't laughing any longer during my lessons; either I had more control over my emotions or I didn't find anything to laugh about. I expected fast results. I wanted to talk normally by now. I got frustrated.

The standard clock time had turned back an hour at the end of October, making the evenings darker…and longer. I grew bored.

I thought it might be time to be discharged because of my lack of progress. I was ready for the big conference someday soon and the news that I was to be discharged. I had to agree with them – it would not be unexpected.

* * *

I was used to the unexpected. When my girlfriend who was a teacher, my first real love, broke up with me: that was unexpected. My stroke was unexpected but by that time, the unexpected had become…well…expected.

In 1979 I started my family practice or general practice, the common name back then, in Saint John. On the second day after opening up my door to patients, a gentleman came in complaining of a sore neck. After examining his neck, I felt it was probably a muscular or ligamentous strain, so I prescribed heat, exercises, and a mild analgesic.

The next day or the day after he returned, complaining that his neck muscles felt weak – he could hardly hold his neck up by the evening. *No* I thought, *it couldn't be? – Myasthenia Gravis? – I just started – my first week!* I was afraid I was reading too much into the symptoms – over-diagnosing. And if I were wrong – I'd be awhile living that one down among my peers. *You know that new doc – what's his name…Jennings, that's it – well he calls me the*

other day – he's been in practice three days – and he's got this
guy with a sore neck and guess what he thinks he
has...Myasthenia Gravis...ha-ha-ha-ha... I thought I'd have him
come back tomorrow: I was uneasy.

The next day he had a new and more ominous complaint.
"You know, last night, not only did my neck muscles get weak, but I
had a hard time closing my eyes."

That did it! Egg on my face or not I had to get this fellow into
hospital under a specialist. I was wrong about the specialist. After I
introduced myself and explained that I wanted him to see my patient
and that he probably needed admission today, there was scepticism
in his voice, that drawn out, lower to high pitched, "Yes?" But when
he heard my patient's presenting complaints, he was most
accommodating and agreed to meet him at the hospital later that
day.

None too soon, for that same night he had a Myasthenia
crisis: he stopped breathing and had to be intubated and put on a
respirator. That gentleman eventually recovered and remained well
controlled, and lived many years before passing away from heart
disease.

I never saw another case of Myasthenia Gravis in the next
twenty years. What were the odds of me encountering this disease in
the first week? That was just a tune-up for the unexpected.

I expected terminal diseases in my patients – everybody has
to die of something – but it is always unexpected when it happens to
my patient who has become more than a patient, a friend. It was
impossible to treat Mrs. Nicholson for fifteen years and not become
her friend, making it shocking and unexpected when I diagnose a
terminal disease.

Medicine is fraught with unexpected diseases; it is the rule
more than the exception. The greatest, unexpected event that
happened to me came when least expected, and it resulted in the
most grief.

The flu vaccination has reduced morbidity. It is especially valuable for the elderly and anyone with a chronic illness. I was convinced of the benefit and therefore strongly advised it for my geriatric and chronically ill patient population. I had also started to use the vaccine personally and had not experienced influenza for a number of years, despite my repeated exposure to the virus.

Nearly four hundred people wished to receive the vaccine, and for a number of years I had been giving the vaccines on two or three specific days – Flu Days we called them. My nurse and I spent the whole day giving flu shots and not seeing any booked patients.

On this day she drew up the first ten injections; put five in my room; and we started. We worked hard throughout the whole day; I occasionally stopped when I had to see a patient for another illness that presented that day, but for the most part nothing unusual occurred.

The following evening, a Friday night, I received a disturbing call from the Emergency Physician, informing me that Mrs. Davis had just been admitted to ICU (intensive care unit) in septic shock, and her arm, where she had received the flu injection, was grossly swollen and red. I felt my stomach twist into a knot.

When I saw her, she was in a coma and her kidneys had shut down – renal failure. This occurs as the blood pressure falls and there is not enough pressure to perfuse the kidney. In this case the kidney got bombarded with too many toxins from the infection. The doctors were giving her a combination of antibiotics, uncertain of what pathogen caused this massive infection.

I felt terrible; the arm was obviously the site of the primary infection; it was grossly swollen and red from her shoulder to her fingertips. The injection had to be the source. How did we contaminate a needle? And with what? My worst nightmare came to fruit: I was the cause of a patient's illness and possible death. One of the principles of the Hippocratic Oath: 'first do no harm', had been violated. My face and manner probably betrayed the guilt I felt, but the worst was yet to come.

I was paged to call the Emergency Department. The physician on duty in the Emergency that day asked me, "What were you using as a needle for those flu shots you gave?"

I thought he was joking, so I answered with a nervous wisecrack, but he wasn't being funny: there were two more of my patients in Emergency with swollen, red arms from the injections. They were not nearly as toxic as Mrs. Davis, but after consultation with specialists, they were admitted under my care with IV penicillin.

I was not on call that Saturday but I stayed in the hospital as more of my patients rolled in. My anxiety level increased as each patient presented: *I had injected over 200 people!* I admitted five people that day with a cellulitis (skin infection) of the arm.

I obtained very little sleep that night as thoughts pressured my brain: How many patients have been affected? How did it happen? I went over and over our procedure in the office. Am I using the right antibiotic? What if a patient ignores the symptoms, thinking it's just a reaction from the flu shot, and seeks help too late? I knew what I had to do: call everyone and check their arm even if they had only a minor mark.

The next day, Sunday, I started calling patients from the master list. Thankfully, Leah, my receptionist was always thorough and kept a schedule of when each patient came in. I spent the day on the phone, checking patients in my office, running up to the hospital to admit more people and checking those admitted. In the end, eight patients were admitted under my care, one patient who lived in Fredericton was admitted up there, and Mrs. Davis in ICU, making a total of ten people. It could have been worse.

By Sunday I observed a trend in those infected. They had been the first ten injected that day. My nurse had drawn up the first ten needles – you get ten injections from one vial. She gave five and I gave five. Therefore it was not the way we injected but either the contamination occurred when my nurse drew up the needles or the vial was contaminated to begin with.

It would have been difficult for her to contaminate ten needles or syringes especially when you swab the top of the vial with alcohol before withdrawing the vaccine. This technique is used thousands of times every day and is pretty foolproof. No, my suspicion was the vial. I thought it must have been contaminated to begin with.

The vial of flu vaccine, enough for ten injections, came at that time with a metal top that you pulled off. The rubber top on the vial was exposed around the circumference of the metal flip top. It seemed to me that a defect in the rubber top might have occurred, exposing the vaccine to possible contamination, or (more of a long shot) someone could maliciously have injected a vial without removing the metal flip top. But the vaccine is immersed in a preservative that prevents the possibility of contamination, making this an unlikely event also. The vial had been discarded, so unfortunately this could never be verified.

Dr. Fan was the Public Health Officer in Saint John at the time and he was a great help to me in helping me track down where this infection could have come from. (Sadly, a few years later Dr. Fan died in a motor vehicle accident in Nova Scotia.) Eventually the Chief Medical Health Officer of New Brunswick became involved and then the National Public Health Office in Ottawa. They investigated my office, procedures, the trail of the vaccine, but no definite conclusions were reached.

All my patients recovered. The bacteria was cultured and found to be Streptococcus – a very common bacteria, often the cause of sore throats but occasionally very nasty when introduced into the skin. Penicillin intravenously worked, but I had many anxious days watching red and swollen skin lines stop advancing and slowly recede.

Mrs. Davis lived, but at a price. She lived maybe two days with no urinary output and then, when all seemed hopeless, her kidneys started to function. She continued to make progress and gave me great hope; however, when she regained consciousness she was deaf. She lost her hearing from the Gentamicin they gave her when she first came into the hospital. At high levels, Gentamicin is toxic to the nerve used for hearing, and because she had no urinary output the drug stayed around too long.

I have been humbled by medicine many times in my twenty years of practice but never as much as by this event. It was a very stressful time for me, but I was pleased I handled it as well as I did. However it was six months later and soon after Dave died of low platelets that I suffered a depression. Whatever defences I used to deal with stress finally snapped.

When I had this stroke, I did cry to God, "Why me?" but it didn't last long – I was used to the unexpected.

* * *

Jenny, my dog, was not doing well. She was not eating and getting thinner. After a couple of weeks it was apparent to us that Jenny was very sick. Jill took her to the Vet who found her dehydrated and with elevated liver enzymes. They admitted her into the animal hospital for IV hydration. I felt useless to Jenny during this time; I couldn't comfort her or take her to the Veterinarian myself. The animal kingdom instinctively chooses the strongest as their leader with good reason: Jenny knew I would be no asset to her in time of crisis, and I proved her intuition right.

Eventually Jenny journeyed to the Atlantic Veterinary College where they did a liver biopsy and found she had a type of hepatitis. I am happy to report that Jenny is doing well and is very healthy after taking steroids for a period of time.

Friends and family continued to provide support and encouragement and I returned the favour by being a great form of entertainment. At the dinner table I provided the comic relief between courses as I sometimes regurgitated food through my nose. There is a lot of space in my nose to accomplish this feat. My palate was incompetent and my swallowing technique was crude; food could travel up into my nose just as easy as going down my esophagus. My kids have seen it all: spaghetti, tuna, soup, vegetables, and other foodstuffs appearing from my nose. Colin and Beth were mostly grossed out, but my youngest, Tara, found it hilarious. The more she laughed the worse I laughed making the scene quite ridiculous: spaghetti (or worse) hanging out my nose while we all laughed and couldn't stop.

My startle response provided another action that created hilarity. It is a primitive response that resides in the brainstem and mine was maladjusted. This is a common complaint among brainstem stroke survivors: a sudden noise produces movements in our limbs and body we didn't think we were capable of. Jenny warns the family when someone is coming in or approaching an outside door by barking. Once I sat in my chair drinking when Jenny yelped as someone opened the door; the drink flew out of my hand, all over the room, the person next to me, the Christmas tree, and me. My mother came to the door once (no barking dog) and I threw my coffee (not hot, thankfully) into Jill's face.

We laughed about my voice; we laughed about Jill showing me how to walk (it looked like a goose-step); we laughed about Jenny ignoring me, no matter what I did to please her; we laughed about my attempts to sit, stand, walk; we laughed about my laugh; we laughed a lot. It is why I liked being home: they helped me forget the pain of failure. We didn't intentionally say, "Let's not be gloomy about Dad's misfortune; let's be positive." It just happened naturally. I hope it was a result of the spirit we share as a family.

Sometimes we have a choice: we can continue to feel miserable or we can make the effort and be happy. And sometimes it does take effort; it is too easy to wallow in self pity. Sometimes you have to take charge of your live and choose to live happy instead of sad. I didn't have to choose to be happy, my family made that choice for me.

Humour has always been an important way for me to stay positive. I wasn't funny. I could never tell a joke but I appreciated humour, and it is much easier being pleasant than serious. We used humour to our advantage in my family; I used it in my practice – especially with children. Children are special. They have an inner happiness and I loved being around them to catch just a bit of their joy. I do miss them. And sometimes I didn't have to find humour; humour just found me…

* * *

I tried to explain to my patients procedures that I was about to perform on them. I did this early in my career and perhaps I went into too much detail – confused, more than helped them.

It was my habit to explain to ladies – especially women I had not seen before – how I would be doing their breast exam. Routinely I said, "Now I wish to do a breast exam today. I want you to remove your bra, then I will have you put your arms over your head while I observe the symmetry of your breasts, looking for lumps and bumps before I actually have you lie down and I palpate or feel for lumps and bumps."

Kind of a mouthful and after awhile the brain gets lazy; it starts to take shortcuts, not thinking about what is being said. That can get you into trouble.

One day, an elderly lady came in for a check-up and I noticed she was due for a breast exam. I had never seen this lady before so I started my little spiel about how I would be performing the breast exam, but I missed a vital part of my speech. "Now I wish to do a breast exam today. I want you to remove your bra, put *it* over your head while I observe the symmetry of your breasts, looking for lumps and bumps before I actually have you lie down and I palpate or feel your breasts for lumps and bumps."

I must have been tired or in a hurry because I did not realize my brain had left out the part, "your arms". I left the room while she undressed and I went to talk to another patient. On my return – yep, you guessed it – there sat a woman looking like a demented Mickey Mouse; bra cups were resting on her head, pointing straight up in the air.

I realized immediately what I had said, and being embarrassed for her, I discreetly removed the bra from her head and proceeded on with my examination as though nothing unusual had transpired. It was later, after all my patients had been seen for the day and I sat in my office by myself busily doing paperwork, that the image hit me again. I howled with laughter. The absurdity of the moment hit me and I could imagine her evaluation of my performance with her friends over tea some afternoon, "You know that new doctor, the one who took over for Dr. Grant… What's his name…Jennings…Yes, that's it…well, he has the strangest ideas…"

Years ago, I had a patient, a student nurse, who had a very irritating problem: she had a malodorous vaginal discharge. I tried different creams and lotions; I tried treating her for infections I didn't see, like Candidiasis or Trichomonas; I cultured; I sent her to specialists. She kept coming back. Everything I prescribed failed; every culture was negative; every specialist's idea failed – they were stumped. I was frustrated. I had known this girl since she was small and I knew she wasn't exaggerating her symptoms: she had a very embarrassing problem. (I now know she probably had a bacterial vaginitis, which has a simple cure, but we didn't know about this condition back then.)

Every visit was the same and I ran out of ideas, but one day she came in quite cheerful. It was time for her routine pap smear. She never said a thing about a malodorous vaginal discharge but the temptation was too great, I had to ask her about the problem.

"Oh, thanks for asking, but it seems to have gone away – about a week now. I don't know how? Nothing I did."

I had hoped for this – a sudden cure – the problem to vanish as quickly and as mysteriously as it came. I commenced the pelvic exam by introducing the speculum into her vagina; I opened it up slowly and there to my astonishment was a huge wad of pink chewing gum lying under her cervix at the top of the vagina. The speculum shook as I tried not to laugh. I asked my nurse for the long forceps and I quietly removed the prize. Unmistakable – it was Double Bubble; I remembered that smell from childhood.

I was too embarrassed for her to mention it to her. What advantage would there be in telling her? Anyway, I had a new cure for malodorous vaginal discharge: Double Bubble.

How the chewing gum got there, I was never brave enough to ask; the truth is probably not nearly as exciting as my imagination. I have heard of putting your chewing gum on the bedpost overnight but never…

Mark had venereal warts on his penis. I think he was rather proud of them – a badge of courage – although we all know the warts are more, a badge of stupidity. These warts are sexually transmitted and easily preventable by wearing a condom. It irritated me because no matter how hard I preached to my young patients about using a condom until they married, or how often they heard the message in school or via the media, they still came in with sexually transmitted diseases and unwanted pregnancies. Condylomata or venereal warts are serious, because the virus that causes them is responsible for the development of cervical cancer.

I often used electrodesiccation to remove warts from the penis. This method involves burning the warts via an electrical spark after freezing.

Mark was confident, and lay back with his arms behind his head as I busily removed the warts from his penis. "Tell me, Doc, is that your Mercedes out front?"

"No, Mark. That belongs to the cardiologist beside me."

"Well is that your BMW?"

"No, that's the other cardiologist beside me. I own the grey little Escort out there."

Mark pondered this information for a while and then said, "Not much money in dink warts, eh Doc!"

The above stories are true and only a sample of twenty years in practice. Each doctor has many to tell and we often swap them at get-togethers. Humour is important. We can't always take things seriously – we have to laugh at ourselves. Laughter *is* the best medicine. The happiest patients I had were those who laughed easily. Seems like an obvious statement, but being happy does not always mean being healthy.

Roy was religious and always smiling; he always had a joke, was always grateful, courteous, and so it was painful to me when he developed cancer of the pancreas. He kept his smile even as his health deteriorated. He didn't need to be healthy to smile. He believed in God and was sure of his afterlife. It wasn't easy to keep happy; the pain was intense; I had to start a morphine pump, which is a small automatic device that attaches to a person and delivers morphine at prescribed doses and times. He was constipated, nauseated, and weak. Yet Roy smiled.

One day when I came to visit, Roy was outside. His condition had deteriorated and I had had to increase the morphine. I had expected to find Roy in bed, emaciated, half aware of his own presence. Instead I found him on a stool by his fence, painting.

"It makes me happy to paint my fence," he said.

I could not stop smiling along with him as I watched him paint. He told me a story about him dancing at his church, in the way only French Canadians can, and all the old ladies laughed and gave him kisses. And he continued to paint. He didn't need me that day. I would never be able to help him more than that fence.

He died a week later. It's not easy to leave this world but no one left it with more grace than Roy.

I think my patients taught me to laugh more, not to take life so seriously. It's easier to smile than frown, laugh than cry – it is a choice. I thank all my past and present patients for giving me more laughs than tears, more smiles than frowns, and inner peace. Humour and laughter were the medicines I needed as I lay in my cocoon.

* * *

Butterflies emerge from cocoons; I was anything but a butterfly. And I was only partially out of my cocoon. I feared my dream of walking out of the Rehabilitation Centre would not be realized. I knew I was lucky to have gotten this far, but we always dream and want more.

A fellow came to visit me who was a brainstem stroke survivor. He had heard of me and had travelled quite a distance to see me, perhaps to lend support. I was most appreciative that he went through all that trouble. I could see he only wanted to do good but there was a part of me that was jealous, for he walked and talked normally. I learned from him that, by this chronological stroke age, he was walking. He was one of the few brainstem stroke survivors who regain perfectly normal function, that I had read about in the medical articles Dr. Milczarek had given me. (I suspect the stats may change, as there will be more people with less damage as TPA becomes more widely available.) I knew I would never be like him; my progress had slowed down enormously.

Family Conferences were held periodically for patients in Stan Cassidy. The whole team (doctor, nurse, OT, etc.) met with the patient and family to discuss progress, problems, and plans. When my conference came up at the end of November, I entered it with mixed feelings. I didn't want to leave Stan Cassidy; I knew I would never get such intensive therapy as an outpatient in Saint John. Yet I knew my progress was slowing and I expected the news of discharge.

They wanted me to stay. They agreed my progress had slowed down but they felt I was still progressing. I was happy they felt I could still make progress and I wanted to stay – I wasn't sure they were right. Probably all stroke survivors feel a sense of let-down at this phase. The quick recovery phase has ended but that is not to say recovery has finished. The recovery from this point on was painful, slow, and frustrating. It took more effort, will, and determination, but it happened. Besides, Dr. Milczarek informed me that there was a new drug being released for spasticity and we could try it after Christmas. This excited me: tone was my enemy. It held me imprisoned in my body. I didn't know what the ransom was but I was willing to pay whatever price.

Stan Cassidy Centre closes for three weeks over Christmas, so I would be home for a while. It would give me a good break from the routine of institutionalized care and a chance to be with my family.

I extended my right arm for the first time in physiotherapy shortly after the meeting; it had been in a bent elbow position for months. The biceps muscle was contracted continuously, making it hard for the muscles behind the upper arm to work (the extensors). I felt as though it were a sign, saying: 'Don't give up. Progress can still happen'.

Other things improved: turning or pivoting while holding the walker, and I could take some shirts off myself. (This surprised me. I thought there must be some formalized set of instructions for disabled people to remove shirts independently, like the directions in making a Windsor knot in a necktie. No such luck. There are some rules like taking the affected arm out last, or in my case, the least affected arm, but overall it's brute strength. Pull, grab, grunt, pull again and basically that's it; not very scientific, just a lot of work.)

I could open my mouth a little more and the tip of my tongue could be seen when I attempted to stick it out. But I gritted my teeth due to the spasm in my jaw muscles so much, my canine teeth had worn down flat instead of having pointed tips. Stiffness was especially bothersome in the morning; my whole body would be stiff including my masseter muscles. I could barely open my mouth, and even my vocal cord muscles were tight, making my voice inaudible or squeaky at best.

I had better control over my emotions. Another student nurse was assigned to my care for a week, and near the end of her time with me she had questions for me as part of her course. This time I didn't cry – she did. I was able to talk about sex, my kids, my wife, God, and other topics without bawling. I wasn't crying when I left home after a weekend any more. I could feel sad without crying or happy without laughing. It had taken six months and I wasn't entirely normal, but having control of my emotions made me feel whole. I was more human. I didn't have control over my body but at least I had control of my mind, thoughts, and now my emotions.

I became excited as the time for Christmas break neared. I needed a change, but I was also worried about how much of a burden I would be to Jill. I was scared to find out.

* * *

Jill was more anxious than I. She felt the stress of being totally responsible for my care and not having backup. The kids were still at school or university, so during the day she had no helpers. I knew this was a hurdle she would have to face: taking a loved one home from institutionalized care and having to accept their total care. I had observed this many times over the years in my own practice. A loved one is in hospital for many months after a life-altering illness and finally the time comes for the patient to go home; the family then starts to make excuses why he or she can't go home, or they put up roadblocks in the way of discharge. Underneath these obstacles the truth is: they are afraid. Once the patient is home and settled, things usually work out; anxieties are relieved, and the patient often improves by being home. I was very confident in Jill's ability to look after me, but I was worried I would prove to be too much care for her and would need a full-time attendant. I really didn't think so but the possibility was in the back of my mind.

I shook Jill's confidence the first day we were home by falling. She was helping me up from bed after my stretching exercises when my legs gave out. I didn't hurt myself; it actually felt good to be on the floor, as silly as that sounds. But Jill was very concerned. She tried to help me up but I was useless and proved to be too heavy. It was noon and a friend of mine, Peter Flemming, worked nearby. He and his wife, Lynn, came over and helped me up. That was the only time I fell in those three weeks. Unfortunately it had to be the first day.

Jill did fine, as I knew she would, but I was a burden. We got rid of the hospital bed and for the first time in six months, I shared my bed with Jill. It felt so good to be back with her. I had missed her presence: the hugs, the goodnight kiss, the talks before sleep, her breathing.

I was as excited as a newly wed (well, maybe not quite that excited) to be going to bed with Jill. I loved her so and it was great, but I broke the enchantment by requesting a turn every few hours.

At Stan Cassidy they came to turn me when I called. I had dispensed with the pillow between my knees and could sleep with my head lower, but I still required a pillow at my back or I would fall over. Usually I asked them to turn me twice a night, some nights more, some less, but I had no ability to turn myself. At home I had to wake Jill up two or three times a night. I realized we couldn't do this forever, so when I returned to Stan Cassidy after Christmas, I wanted to focus on turning in bed by myself. I tried to stay in one position, but my hips became so sore I had to move.

I was afraid Jill was becoming tired, and I feared what effect my stroke would have on our relationship. I knew the statistics: 50% of marriages end in divorce after stroke. It is not hard to see why it happens: sometimes a stroke changes the survivor's personality because of where in the brain the damage occurred; sometimes the survivor's personality changes because he or she is mad at the world; sometimes the caregiver's personality changes because he or she is mad at being given this new role they didn't ask for. There are a lot of reasons why marriages break down. Jill and I had had a solid partnership up until now – we hardly ever argued. But relationships can change.

I was incapable of turning and cuddling with Jill as we went to sleep. I was incapable of talking about the day or planning for tomorrow. I was incapable of turning over and kissing Jill goodnight. I was incapable of tenderly making love. Instead, it seemed to me I was a burden on Jill. She had to help me into bed, position me, and then I broke her sleep by having to turn throughout the night. I hated my new role. It made me feel reduced; I was no longer 'the protector', 'the man', instead Jill now had to protect me.

I worried about our future, and one night that worry turned to anger. There was nothing Jill could do to please me and I lashed out. I wanted to be 'the man'. I wanted to turn and hug Jill, stroke her back, cuddle. Instead I had to wait for a hug, for a kiss, and I had no way of showing her I wanted to make love: I either just had to say it, which sounded so cold and contrived to me, or Jill had to initiate the desire.

Like always Jill saw through my anger and didn't react with anger but with tenderness. We talked and I realized what was wrong: my role had changed and I had to accept it. It is hard sometimes to accept and I have no magic formula for you, the stroke survivor, but you have to adapt somehow to these changes. Love is worth the effort to accept change.

* * *

I was very happy that Christmas despite my 'blow-up' that one night. In fact, it was probably my happiest Christmas ever. I was thankful to be alive and to be spending another Christmas with my family. CBC radio came to interview me and I told them I was happy and my spirit felt light. Yeah, that's how I felt, if asked again – light.

No burdens were weighing me down; I was giddy with happiness; I was in love with life; my spirit felt light.

I always loved the Christmas season but that year had special meaning for me. The carols, old and familiar as they were, seemed fresh; the Christmas lights seemed brighter, and the Christmas tree scent was more poignant. People seemed merrier; our parents more dear; and my children more lovable. Jill was my soul mate; it was impossible to feel closer to any other human being.

Friends visited; I went to church; I went on outings. I visited old patients; I met old patients at malls; I visited nursing homes I used to attend. I went to the old City Market: the smells and sights assaulted me. I was tormented by the food on display – I was still only able to manage pureed food at this time, and all the fruits, baked goods, cheeses, and meats were taunting me.

I tasted a beer for the first time since my stroke. I loved the taste of beer, yet I had forgotten the smell and I spent five minutes lingering over my glass, just smelling it. The alcohol content on my first sip sent my throat into spasms and I coughed and hacked most of it up. I took a smaller sip on my next attempt, and reluctantly my throat accepted and swallowed it. But the taste! My taste buds did the 'Hurley Gurley'. It was the taste experience of the very first beer you ever had, only pleasant. Since then, I don't often drink beer – it is still difficult to swallow and I have to sip it. Besides, even one beer slurs my speech and makes me weak. Oh well, just another thing in my life I've had to adjust to.

Speaking of adjustments, I had to watch my family pick out a Christmas tree and then erect it and decorate it. That was painful. I tried not to say anything, but honestly that was the worst looking tree I'd ever seen. And then I had to keep quiet as I watched Jill and Colin struggle to erect the tree – they will probably say I didn't keep quiet but that's not true! I had loved helping out with the Christmas decorating. It was never a chore; it was festive, a family thing, and I missed partaking in that joy. Oh well, just another thing…Adjusting!

Always adjusting!

Every Christmas Eve I'd read to the kids *T'was the Night Before Christmas* and *How the Grinch Stole Christmas.* On the Grinch, I used a Grinchy voice when he spoke: I didn't have to improvise that year. I didn't have the stamina to read the whole poem or story, so we took turns reading a page. We laughed forever that night. Even my son Colin, by then a young man of twenty, took part. Young men have a hard time showing emotions, especially with their parents; I was appreciative of his involvement.

My kids went to bed; it was now time for Mom and Dad to act like Santa. I only watched as Jill laid out our gifts to the children. I was feeling pretty useless but that didn't dampen my spirit; my so-called adjustments only made me more determined to improve so I could be more helpful next Christmas season.

It was a white Christmas. The snow had come early that year and had stayed. It seems less cold when the snow comes. It is easier to watch the grass and trees with snow on them; they look warmer. I felt warm in spirit that Christmas morning as I watched my family opening up gifts, saying 'Thank you!' and 'Oh, I love this!' They had to help me open up gifts but they seemed genuinely delighted in doing that, turning them over in my lap or holding an article of clothing up to my chest so I could see what it looked like. We smiled a lot that morning and I was thankful to be there.

Later that day my parents came over for Christmas dinner. The smell of the turkey cooking all day had driven me crazy. I didn't want pureed turkey again; I wanted the whole enchilada. I knew I couldn't, so Jill compromised with me; instead of pureed, she diced up the turkey fine. I had mashed potatoes, squash, pees, carrots, jellied salad, dressing, and turkey. It actually looked like food. I choked a bit over the turkey but it was worth it; it was a big step for me and I celebrated with a little wine, which I promptly choked on. I was thankful and thanked God for allowing me this moment with my family.

A few days later Jill's father and mother, Dr. Bill and Adele Moreside; her three sisters and their husbands and our nieces and nephews from Prince Edward Island and Halifax came for a day. I had more family to celebrate with and we laughed and joked like always; nothing had changed really. The only difference was that I was in a wheelchair. I couldn't talk as well, but they treated me like Shawn. They didn't patronize me or spare me the brunt of their jokes. They seemed to feel comfortable with me and I with them. I was sorry when they had to head home; their visit had brought energy and with their absence I was left to contemplate my return to Stan Cassidy.

I wanted to return because I wanted to improve, and now I had new goals, but still, I had to leave my family. The three weeks had flown by, and the seven months before that had crawled. *Seven months ago I was happily running down those stairs on my way to work. The day was beautiful, full of promise...Oh why? Why?* I remembered those days lying in the NICU – smothering, hot, daydream-like, unfocused. I couldn't believe that was my experience. It seemed unreal and at the same time very much real. Thinking. Thinking. Always thinking. I want to be rid of those memories and I know I never will be. Locked In. A life I never want to think about but I have no choice: it was my life.

Heading back to Stan Cassidy made me reflect about my situation. I wished I could stay home and forget about it, but I was driven to improve. I had hope, and with the introduction of the new medication my hope had foundation. *I feel I'm going to walk. I will.*

CHAPTER 12 – JANUARY – MARCH

On my return to Stan Cassidy, Todd and I again shared a room. This pleased me; I found him to be a very pleasant young man and we shared many a laugh.

I quickly returned to the routine: the wakeup call, the therapy schedule board, the meals, the long evenings, and finally the bed routine. The white cement walls felt colder, the bathrooms smaller, and the cafeteria more sterile. However the staff still glowed with warmth and it was not long before Denis had me laughing or Louise had me smiling and I shook off my melancholy mood.

The nursing staff was special: each person brought me something from their own personality that helped me. I could write about each one and their unique gifts they brought to work each day. They became almost maternal (or paternal) as they taught me how to wash my face again, shave, brush my teeth, and all the personal tasks my own mother had once taught me. Some were better than others at teaching; some brought humour, some did not; some brought stories of their families, some were private; some were happy in their own lives, some were not – but they all brought kindness and compassion and smiles.

I still had my main girls, Beth, Mereille, and Doreen, and they were happy to see I hadn't lost any function in the three weeks I was home. My daughters, Beth and Tara, had done my stretching exercises most days, giving Jill a break. I was proud and touched having my daughters perform physiotherapy on my limbs. They were not timid in touching their Dad. They pulled, lifted, twisted, and pushed my limbs with great gusto.

I entered my therapies with a renewed sense of determination. I could tell my speech was improving at a slow rate and I wanted to work harder on my breath support and pronunciation.

I had two main goals I wanted physiotherapy and OT to help me with: I wanted to be able to turn in bed by myself and I wanted to be independent moving my wheelchair. Secretly, I wanted to walk but I kept this to myself. I thought it might be possible if the new medication reduced my tone, but I didn't want to verbalize my hopes; it's harder to act nonchalant in failure if everyone knows you failed.

It wasn't hard to keep quiet; no one knew what I was saying anyway. Tracy was a new speech language pathologist I was introduced to; apparently Beth had been covering for Tracy during her pregnancy leave. I still saw Beth once a week but I had Tracy daily. Tracy was a very pretty young woman whose appearance didn't soften her approach; she was every bit as hard a taskmaster as Beth.

After weeks of individual sessions, Tracy decided to try me in a group. I still saw Beth weekly for private work but I went to group twice a week. Most of the exercises that the speech therapists gave me to increase my breath support were difficult to do daily – to stay motivated. The improvements weren't weekly, barely monthly; it is hard to repeat exercises if you get no positive reward – no visual gains. This was not unique to speech therapy; all rehabilitation is like this to some degree. You have to keep reminding yourself that, at the very least, you're not losing and if you give up, it is a definite – you won't succeed.

I was still stubborn about getting a power chair. I tried over Christmas to travel independently in my home, but after a time – measured by my tolerance for frustration – I called Jill or one of the kids for help. Did I try long enough? If they weren't there, would I have succeeded or would I be there still? Questions like these bothered me, and for these reasons I had not ordered a power chair even by this time.

My arm was rigid and so was my body. I continued to be unable to stand, sit, or turn in bed. Tone. Tone. Tone.

I was no further ahead with my ability to walk. Jill, Betty,

Doreen, and Mereille continued as my entourage as I 'walked' through the gym. They stayed positive and Mereille saw little improvements, but I saw little to be joyful about. I did start to swing my back leg up to meet my other leg, but it was occasional and took a lot of effort. My legs refused to bend, relax; they stayed rigid, and unless they loosened up a bit, I would never walk.

I eagerly awaited the introduction of the new medicine to my drug schedule: it could be my ticket to freedom.

*   *   *

Zanaflex was the new antispasmodic drug that held up my hopes. It had just been approved for use in Canada and I was eager to start. It has a nasty side effect of drowsiness, so it has to be started slowly and then the dosage titrated upward until the desired effect is reached, or the maximum dose. Some people are not bothered by drowsiness or other side effects, some people accommodate to the side effects, and some people never adapt to the drug. The idiosyncratic nature of drug behaviour in the human body was always readily apparent to me in treating hypertension.

Treating hypertension can be lifesaving, and at the very least lowering blood pressure reduces a risk factor for many diseases. However hypertension as a disease is usually asymptomatic; it is difficult giving a drug to an individual who feels well and subjecting them to a potential side effect. The trick always is to find a drug that causes no side effects for that individual. The physician and the patient have to work together to reach that goal of treating hypertension effectively while minimizing the side effects. And sometimes some side effects have to be accepted for the greater benefit.

Dr. Milczarek started me on a low dose as recommended. For the first few days, I was drowsy; I had expected this but usually my body adapted to drugs quickly. This time it didn't. After a few days I continued to be drowsy, but I implored Dr. Milczarek to increase the dose anyway. The drowsiness increased. I could barely keep my eyes open as Betty and Esmond stretched my limbs after breakfast. I often fell asleep for short periods and then awoke as they reached my pain threshold for the stretched limb.

My voice, which had been improving, became slurred and unintelligible until the drug wore off. And Zanaflex was not reducing my tone enough to produce a beneficial effect upon my function.

I held on for three weeks. I was determined to make it work. I had such great hope for recovery using Zanaflex, and now those hopes were being tested.

Don't get me wrong. I wasn't expecting Zanaflex would cure me. I knew it would not take the place of hard work, but I hoped it would prove to be a valuable aid – reduce the tone – thereby enabling me to work spastic limbs. If anything, the drowsiness and tiredness was worsening, not improving with time, so reluctantly I asked Dr. Milczarek to take me off Zanaflex.

I did not realize what a fog I had been in for the three weeks I was on Zanaflex until I came off it. Zanaflex is a very good drug for some people. It has made a tremendous difference in the lives of people who can take it. My experience was not great, but I have no hesitation recommending it to another patient. I would caution an individual of potential side effects, but that would not prevent me from prescribing it.

Dr. Milczarek decided to increase my Baclofen (another antispasmodic I was on) to higher dosages, so I still had hope something might help reduce my tone. Maybe even time might help reduce the tone. Baclofen made me drowsy too, but not to the extent Zanaflex did. We went up to recommended maximum dose and then beyond, but it never reduced the tone in my muscles significantly.

I did not give up on Zanaflex over the year; I tried it five more times and each time the results were the same: drowsiness – tiredness. I wanted so much for something to work – reduce my tone and I'd do it! After the fifth time I had to accept it: the drug and

I didn't mix.

There are other ways to reduce tone, which we are exploring, but I've learned not to set my hopes so high. If it helps: great. If it doesn't: oh well.

Another drug that concerned me was Imovane. That was the sleeping medication I started using early on in my illness. As you remember, my sleeping mechanism went awry with my stroke, and it was awhile before we found a sleeping pill that worked.

Dr. Milczarek assured me that my insomnia would resolve with time. I had many patients who had become dependent on sleeping pills (not by me!) and then they develop tolerance to their drug – needing more, or stronger medication – and so the struggle ensued. Sleeping medication should be prescribed for short-term use only. I was determined dependence would not happen to me.

In the fall, I had started to cut down Imovane to half a pill. After my body had accommodated to that reduction and I was still sleeping, I stopped it. My body had repaired itself; I slept well and wasn't dependent on medication.

*   *   *

I walked poorly during the first of February with Mereille. Doreen concentrated on my 'sit to stand' ability and I failed. My back would still not let me bend enough to keep my weight forward. Still the same problem: when I put effort into using my legs to lift – my back extended, throwing my weight backwards. My brain knew what had to be done but my body didn't listen. No matter how hard I told myself to keep my hips bent and my chest forward, my back extended. I had no control and the harder I tried – the worse I did.

Doreen knew I would gain a lot of independence by being able to stand up on my own. And I was so close. I could get up on my own from a certain height, but not from the level of a bed or wheelchair. Two years later, I cannot stand up independently from these levels, unless I'm holding on to something, and even then it is sometimes risky.

I stood by myself holding onto a bar for the first time in December and like most accomplishments in stroke, I thought this was only the beginning. I thought if I kept working at 'sit to stand', I would progress. Sad to say – it doesn't always work out that way. It is the same old story – you may get discouraged with no improvements but don't give up – then you have failed.

I could not flex my hips, thereby bringing my knees up; I needed this to be able to turn in bed. Mereille helped me flex my hips; I tried rocking my knees back and forth and with great effort, I sometimes turned over, only to have my legs now sticking out straight in extension, my back stiff, and my right arm curled up in protest. From this position Mereille now wanted me to kick my legs over the bed, put my arm under my body and lift myself up into sitting position. The best I could do was smile sweetly at her.

I still didn't have 100% control over my bladder function. I didn't wear adult diapers anymore, but I had urgency – when I had to go, I had to go. One night, I awoke needing to urinate but I could not find the call bell. Before I could awaken Todd for help, I peed my bed. I lay in bed, wet, for a few hours, until some nurses came in to attend to Todd.

I thought I had good control but this belief was shaken when I was incontinent once at home, and once another evening at Stan Cassidy. Two steps forward – one step back. Two steps forward – one step back. Always. Frustrating.

I tried to be independent. One morning after breakfast I went into the bathroom by myself, in my power chair, brushed my teeth, cleaned up a bit, urinated using the urinal, congratulated myself, and headed out. A nurse had closed the door after she had come in for some towels, and now I was stuck. I couldn't bend forward enough to grab the door handle, and the room was too small to turn sideways to the door. The emergency bell was located behind the toilet and I couldn't reach the cord. My voice wasn't loud enough to be heard, so I kept banging into the door with my power chair to be heard. Half an hour later, someone did hear, and came to my rescue.

This happened twice.

Yeah, as you can see, by early February, I was frustrated and disappointed. Disappointed by my inability to use Zanaflex, frustrated by my lack of progress and the events that had transpired. I didn't entertain the thought of giving up, though. I hoped this was just a lull in my progression, but I admit: I was discouraged.

Mereille and Doreen's attitudes were especially important to me during this time. Their humour and positive attitude sustained me.

My discharge date was coming up – February 11 – and I was ready to go. After all I came back to try the Zanaflex – the trial failed, so I thought I was due to go. Dr. Milczarek came to watch me walk and after consultation with Mereille, he concluded he would like me to stay, until the end of March. They had seen some recent improvements and would like to work on them. Apparently, they saw improvements in my walking! I didn't see it but I was more than willing to stay if there was a chance in walking.

Besides, not everything was negative. I moved my right arm up to touch my face for the first time and my left arm was stronger. My balance was terrible but my legs were stronger. I could turn pages better, lift cups to my mouth, wash, shave – all better. My emotions were fully under my control now; I could listen to music again.

*   *   *

Music has always been an important part of my life. I started playing guitar in grade nine when I asked for an electric guitar and amplifier for Christmas from the Sears catalogue. It was an AGS with two pickups (I had no idea what this meant – I think it stands for American Guitar Supply) and a sunburst finish. The amplifier had a whopping five watts, but that would prove to be more than loud enough – according to my parents. The action (the ease of pressing a string to a fret) was horrible, but I was in heaven.

My musical tastes gradually changed from electric to acoustic over the years. I was self-taught, never very good, I didn't try to be good – it was for my enjoyment only and I sounded good enough for me.

In high school my musical tastes were the Beatles, Rolling Stones, and later Led Zeppelin. In my university days I started playing more Cat Stevens, Paul Simon, and Neil Young. I strummed or finger picked the guitar and sang. I never could sing, but my family will tell you it wasn't from lack of trying. I loved playing my guitar and singing. It was what I did to relax.

We bought a piano because Jill plays and we wanted our children to learn. I learned to adapt my knowledge of guitar chords to the piano, play them with my right hand while doing a bass run with my left hand, and singing the melody. I had great fun doing this too, but the guitar was my love. (My kids preferred the guitar – at least I was in my room, by myself!) It was almost a compulsion; I had to feel the guitar neck in my hand at least once a day. I had to pick the darn thing up, even if it was only for five minutes.

I remember working in the office all day, going to the Emergency for an evening shift, coming home at midnight tired, and still picking up the guitar to play something quiet while I unwound. Jill said she could always tell what mood I was in by what I played. If I came home angry or disturbed about something that had occurred, an angry Neil Young song would come out. If I was melancholy, it was bluesy or a quiet Neil Young or Bob Dylan or Paul Simon. If I was happy, she would hear 'Feeling Groovy' by Paul Simon or 'Cinnamon Girl' by Neil Young. I sometimes became studious and a Beatles melody in classical style came out, or I attempted a Michael Hedges or Leo Kottke tune. I enjoyed writing my own songs, too –

never serious, never recorded, often forgotten after a few days, but fun and probably cathartic.

When I was a young man, I vowed I would buy a Martin guitar when I could afford it. And I did. I loved my Martin guitar; I loved the look, sound, feel, even the smell of it. When I had my stroke, it felt strange not to have it near, but it didn't bother me as much as I thought it would. I was unable to play and I accepted this; or at least I thought I did.

One of the good things about coming home on the weekends that first summer, I thought, would be the ability to play my own music. (If you remember, I gave up playing CDs in the portable player because I often ended up with the earphones on my head for a considerable amount of time after the CD finished.) I imagined myself lying back in my own room, listening to my CDs while I waited for my tube feedings to stop. No headphones to contend with and I could listen without disturbing anyone. But Jill put on a Blue Rodeo CD; I settled back for an enjoyable, relaxing few moments, and I started to cry. A familiar guitar part rang out, one that I had tried to emulate many times. It brought back too many memories, too many emotions, all in an instant, and I wasn't ready. My tears were unexpected. I thought I had this music/guitar absence under control. I had to ring my bell for Jill to return and take off the CD. Over the weeks I tried other CDs, other forms of music, but the results were always the same.

At Stan Cassidy, Louise knew I didn't like country music (not that I didn't like it: I had never been exposed to it) so as a joke she often played country music while she helped me prepare for the day. I groaned, pretending to be annoyed, but in actuality I didn't mind it at all. Country music brought back no memories to me; it became a bridge, returning me to tunes I used to listen to.

Now I am trying to use the guitar as a catalyst to awaken memories that may linger in the connection between my brain and my hands. My father-in-law, Dr. Bill Moreside, had a stroke a few years back; he had loss of function in his right hand. He was a good piano player and the inability to play piano was quite devastating. I saw him practice and practice, over and over, until he got that hand back to almost normal function. At first I didn't think he would do it; I was afraid he was frustrating himself with an unobtainable goal. But he did do it.

There seem to be intangibles when we are discussing the mind and music. I can't get my arm around the big body of my Martin guitar, but I am buying an electric guitar, which has a narrow body. I am hoping it will awaken my hand and arm.

Soul seems to want music. I heard music – maybe made up or heard – that first day after wakening from my coma. Classical – did my mind invent it? Or did I *hear* it? While I lay in ICU, I intuitively wanted to listen to nature CDs, even though I'd never listened to them before. My soul seemed to want the tranquility. Music is fascinating; the many varieties; the tones; the way it makes you feel. Music, like love, is food for the soul and my soul seems to be in a feeding frenzy lately. Classical, jazz, pop, rock – anything goes and everything feels right.

*   *   *

At home I requested to be transferred to our sofa less frequently. I grew used to the wheelchair. I no longer felt trapped, confined. This acceptance was a slow process and I wasn't aware of any stages, but I prefer being in my chair now, I find it more comfortable than a normal chair. I have to remind myself to sit on a different chair occasionally. I remembered when I thought I would never get used to a wheelchair. I guess if there is no option the body adapts.

I had no more falls at home and Jill became confident in her ability to look after me. I did sort of fall one more time. One evening when we were practising walking, my pants were wedged and I asked Jill to pull them down. As a joke, Jill did what I requested and pulled my pants and underwear down in one quick swoop. I became weak with laughter and slowly buckled to the floor with Jill trying to keep me up but laughing too hard herself. I ended up sitting on the floor with a bare bottom. After I wrapped myself with a towel, Beth and Tara helped Jill get me up.

We try not to be too jovial while I am on my feet, laughter literally does make my knees go weak.

At home I watched very little television. I guess I was overdosed with those electron images while I was 'locked in'. I exercised, read, or spent time on the computer. I discovered a site on the Internet for stroke survivors to correspond, and specifically a place for brainstem stroke survivors. I found many more like me across North America. Many of the brainstem stroke survivors were young. I found common bonds of experiences; fears and hopes linked us together.

I told you the story about Jim. His wife started to correspond beginning in September, and by January it became apparent to me that he wasn't responding: he continued to be 'locked in'. I found it hard to say anything. It was tough to be encouraging because I knew his hopes of recovery were fading, yet that was what she was asking for. I didn't want to give the 'cold facts' because they were cruel. I saw well-meaning people being too hopeful: 'he'll get better', 'have faith', 'tell him to fight'. I didn't say much but I felt like screaming sometimes, *Maybe he won't get better; it's not his fault if he doesn't improve; sometimes there's nothing to fight with.*

I may have said something to that effect. I didn't want her to lose hope either, but she had to be told his chances for some recovery were dimming as time marched on. Jim could correspond with the eye-gaze board like I had, and by June he made the decision to end his life. He had not improved. He was still quite 'locked in' and decided he didn't want to live in this fashion. He had them stop his tube feeds except for water, and he quietly passed away a few weeks later. No one started a fuss about this being amoral; it was kept quiet apparently, and he was allowed to carry on with his wishes.

I don't know about the morality of suicide anymore. Would it have been more humane to assist him in committing suicide quickly, instead of lingering for a few weeks? Undoubtedly it would have been more humane, but is it moral? Until society or theologians can work this out, we are safer in accepting this form of passive suicide.

I could not help but ask myself, would I have done the same thing as Jim, if I had stayed 'locked in'? I think I would have; I don't think I could have lived only being able to move my eyes: never smiling, unable to kiss, unable to hug. I think those who live this way must be very courageous, perhaps strong in their faith. I don't know if suicide is amoral; I think I would have taken my chances. If God were forgiving perhaps He would understand my reasons for taking my own life. That was hell living like that. Yeah, I would have taken my chances.

I think back to that Saturday in the summer. If I had had a way, would I have committed suicide that day? I don't think so, but my soul was pretty black. That would have been wrong and that is why impulsive suicide has to be prevented. A person may think differently about suicide that stems from depression when they are not depressed. But that is different than a person contemplating suicide who suffers from a terminal or hopeless situation. Surely we've progressed enough in our judgements to be able to distinguish between the two circumstances. Easy enough to say, but I don't think I could actively take another human life. Until we solve this theological question, a passive form of assisting terminal or hopeless situational patients in taking their lives should be advocated.

We put our stories on the web, in the stroke site, and often people will ask us our advice, privately. The danger of the Internet is that people may be posing as someone else. I can tell they often are not sure whether to believe that I am really a doctor. One question I get often is: How did you get through it? I'm sure I've disappointed them with my answer. I tried to think of some clever medical-psychological answer but I could think of none. The answer is quite simple really and one you've heard time after time, in song after song, in sermon after sermon, in whisper after whisper between two lovers – Love.

I hear John Lennon singing, 'Love is the answer...'

*   *   *

Love – so hard to find, so confusing, and so very important in our lives, as I found out. I envy those who find love that lasts forever with their first sweetheart. Before I met Jill, there was one girl I was sure was *the one*. I was astonished to find I was wrong, and even more astonished to find I was to blame for the break-up. Shortly after Debbi and I broke up, I met my new girlfriend, who became a teacher. We broke up after two years and I never figured out why. After I came out of my coma while I was 'locked in', that great mystery of my life was clear to me. I don't know if I was visited by Scrooge-like spirits and shown my transgressions, or another 'God-thing' happened, or if I just had time to think while 'locked in' and revisited my past. The answer was crystal clear – I didn't *call* her once that whole summer. Duh!

I must have thought once you found Love, it stood on its own. Wrong! Love has to be watered to be sustained and grow; stop watering and it will wither. The watering is comprised of kisses, hugs, and acts of kindness, compliments....

Perhaps it was karma; I was to find my soul mate in Jill.

I saw Jill in my first days in medicine. My medical class met one evening for a social event to get to know each other. Before the social we assembled in our large lecture theatre to hear a few students from second year give us their perspective on first year and what text books to buy. Their girlfriends or boyfriends came with them, since the social event was immediately after. They all seemed quite confident – after all they had made it through the first year – but there was one girl who didn't seem as confident as the rest.

She was pretty with dark blonde hair. She was wearing a white top with blue jeans and sneakers. Her face was pleasant to look at; she seemed kind. Her upper lip was different in a pleasant way; I couldn't say how – just different.

There were many other people present but I only remember her. She seemed uncomfortable standing in front of about one hundred medical students. I shared her discomfort; I would have felt the same. She was the girlfriend of one of the second year fellows, but she seemed so unlike him; he seemed so confident as he spoke to us. I liked her – whoever she was. How was I to know? I was looking at my future wife, Jill. She doesn't remember any of it. Darn! I thought she might have spotted me in the crowd of medical students and been enchanted right there – a perfect fairy tale.

I did not see this girl again for over a year, but at a party one night, one of my classmates introduced me to a friend of hers. I recognized her immediately – it was Jill. I had known back then I would like her, and I did. I immediately found her easy to talk to; I felt comfortable in her presence.

She apparently had broken up with her boyfriend but I wasn't sure. Our relationship as friends stayed that way for over a year. Jill worked as a nurse at the Isaac Walton Killam Hospital for Children, and I often saw and spoke to her there. I would see her at parties; we always talked, but I never thought of Jill in any other way than as a friend. Then one day something told me to ask Jill out for a date. We went out with her roommate and her boyfriend (Jill tells me she didn't trust me alone) and we had a wonderful time. She was kind; I had known that from the moment I had seen her in first year.

I was happy – real happy for the first time in years. Jill and I continued seeing each other and before I went into internship we married. We have been married twenty-three years as I'm writing this, and my love for her is still growing. Hopefully I have learned something along the way: hopefully I have remembered to water our love.

I have spent this much time talking about love because love was so important in my recovery. Jill's love for me brought me through. When I was in despair, depressed, and somewhat suicidal, it was Love that brought me out of those depths. Jill didn't have to say much – her touches and smile filled my spirit.

In those early days, as I lay in NICU, her arrival at my bedside filled me with a deep joy. It felt like the joy I experienced the first night I went out with her, only deeper. Just looking at her made me smile. Jill made me believe that any disability I might end up with was inconsequential. Love was my goal in life and I had achieved it. Everything was secondary to the love she and I shared.

I said before I had my stroke and I remembered: "If I die, I die happy." And now that I am living, I am still happy, for I am in love. Love makes my life so full, and it makes me want to try harder. It gives me the desire to improve.

And so, my simple, feeble-sounding answer to the lady who asked me, "How did you get through it?" – Love.

*   *   *

Love was the basis of my acceptance and also my determination to improve. It gave rise to such phrases as: 'I don't know if I will succeed, but I *do* know I won't succeed if I stop trying,' or 'Any movement I gain –however small –is a bonus.' Love was the safety net I used if I failed. What more in this world could I ask for but love?

There are many different types of love that may be just as important as the love Jill and I share: love between child and parent, between siblings, friends, or God. Love for God was important in my recovery.

I went to church as a child. My grandmother made sure I

attended Sunday School at St. Luke's Anglican Church on Main St. in Saint John. Rev. Harry Quinn impressed me: he had white hair and a beard and the robes he wore were magnificent – white and black robes complimented by coloured adornments of brilliant reds or purples or other colours, depending upon the Christian season. And people listened to him. To a shy, scrawny kid, the power and sight of him made quite an impression. Becoming an Anglican priest appealed to me – people would have to listen and I too could wear those fine robes. The status was a temptation to a shy boy.

Religion soon took a backseat in my adolescent years. Like most adolescents, the present became the concern; the immediate was all that mattered. It's hard to think of abstract ideas when you are more concerned with Who am I? What am I doing? What am I going to do in life?

Science had more answers than religion – at least I thought – and I thought less about God. I didn't discount there might be a God but I thought it was not provable and I was into the scientific method. I wanted proof; faith was not enough. I was agnostic – not that I gave it much thought.

Jill started taking the children to Sunday School and I started to go to church again to see them in activities. I started to listen to the Christian message again. Whether I believed in Jesus as divine, at first, made little difference to me; it was the Christian message that was important. The beatitudes were wonderful principles to live your life by, and the Ten Commandments – a good foundation for society.

'Love your neighbour, as you love yourself.' This statement summed up all that was good about Christianity. It also meant to me that, in order to help others you have to think well of yourself. I found this most interesting. The lack of self-esteem is the root of many problems in people, so psychiatry has found out, and Christianity had been saying this all along: you can't be a help to others, if you don't love yourself. Personally, my phobia had battered my self-esteem to smithereens.

In retrospect I think I may not have been agnostic; in retrospect, my phobia precluded my entering a church. I would have been in a sweat entering a building with so many people. This was a major factor why I ignored religion for so long. I returned to religion once I beat my panic disorder.

As I returned to religion and listened to what was said, a curious phenomenon occurred – faith. I had discounted this 'faith', whatever that was, as a young adult, but the more I listened, the more I came to believe that Jesus was divine.

I always believed in the existence of God. I believed He was this omnipotent thing that we can't comprehend and never will until we die. I believed in a life after death, but it too was incomprehensible. I didn't believe God watched us and intervened. I believed either we disappointed Him long ago and He had left us, or He never did intervene in our daily lives.

Although I did believe in the existence of an omnipotent God, there was always a nagging scepticism in the back of my mind: Maybe God never existed; maybe He's a made up myth, made by people long ago to explain our existence, and that story has been added to throughout the years. Or maybe God has gone away. After all, He seemed to speak to chosen people a lot in the Old Testament but not a lot since Jesus. Did we disappoint Him and has He left?

I feel like I've been given the answer to these questions: I *know* God exists. I *knew* this stroke was about to happen. I believe another God-thing happened to me. About a year prior to the stroke, I started to experience weird sensations. They happened about six times prior to the stroke. I would suddenly get a feeling that something drastic was about to happen to my family. I did not know it was a stroke, or even that it would be me the change would occur to, but each time it occurred, I turned to Jill and said, "Something is going to happen to one of us. I just want you to know I love you; and if I die, I die happy. I've done everything I've wanted to do; we've had wonderful kids; and I love you."

The sensations were so clear, so definite – something was going to happen to our family. One time this happened as I walked up my deck on the side of the house. Jill was behind me, and then that feeling happened. I turned to her and told her about what just happened, and how I loved her. Another time it happened as I was falling to sleep. I do not remember the other times because once they happened I soon forgot about them. I did not dwell on it; I was not spooked out by the feelings or necessarily believe them – just one of those freaky things that happen.

I remembered the premonitions soon after I awoke from my coma. I thought, *Holy Cow! Those feelings were true. I believe God warned me. He was preparing me. There is a God and He's watching us. And He cares for us.* This knowledge made me happy, as I lay in NICU. I don't know if it was God who told me, but it was a God-thing anyway.

I feel confident in my soul that I am right: the feeling was so clear. I've never experienced anything comparable to it. If I am right, God is omnipresent. Whoops! I have a lot of explaining to do; I hope He's got a sense of humour.

Jill asks me, if He's so omnipresent, why do atrocities occur, children starve or cancer exist – why? If He knew a stroke was about to occur to you, why didn't He stop it? I don't know the answer to these questions. Maybe He can't change events or maybe He doesn't want to. Maybe there is a higher purpose. I don't know, but I do know God exists.

Sceptics will say I had a near death experience so I have embraced a fable to comfort myself. Knowing God does give me comfort, but I believed in the existence of God before this stroke; I didn't need this experience to make me believe. It solidified my belief in God; it changed my thoughts on how God operates, but I didn't seize the concept of God in an act of desperation.

The feelings I had were clear. Some people will call these feelings premonitions. What is a premonition? Dictionaries tell us –

'an actual warning of something yet to occur' (Collier's) – but nothing about what this phenomenon is. Where does it come from? Do we have another sense? Is there a foreseeable pattern to our lives? I don't think science will ever be able to explain premonition. I think it is God talking to us. I think He talks to us more than we realize. We don't listen or know how.

Intuition. Deepak Chopra believes listening to our intuition, our real intuition, is a stage in knowing God.

Regardless of what you believe about my spiritual experience – 'Hogwash! He's a nice guy but a little flaky' – my religion did afford me comfort in my illness. I often recited Psalm 23 in those first days as I verged on death, 'Even though I walk through the valley of the shadow of death…' It gave me great comfort. I did not fear death. I was not afraid.

The morphine helped; anyone would be calm with morphine on board. But morphine wears off; God doesn't.

I wonder if everyone when they are near death acts a little selfish. I was not worried about Jill and my children; I was not worried about anything.

That curious music was playing in my head and I felt peaceful.

As time went on, I prayed every night. I asked Him for strength; I resisted the temptation to ask for cure. I still ask God for the strength not to give up, but to continue my rehabilitation.

I was a Sunday Christian before. I attended church and prayed with feeling on Sunday, but the rest of the week, I forgot God. I had long ago abandoned my daily prayers I had recited as a child, but now I resurrected them. Since I know God exists, I feel closer to Him, and I know He hears me.

When I finally learned how to turn a page, I started to read the Bible daily, following a devotional guide one of my patients bought for me.

I don't want to make myself out to be someone I'm not. I would be considered a sinner in some circles. I love partying with my friends. I drink beer – not very well – but I do consume alcohol. I laugh at dirty jokes – I find them amusing. Knowing God has not changed me, other than to give me an inner peace.

I have friends who don't necessarily believe in God, but they are good people. They are more 'Christian' than some people I know who never miss church. I imagine God accepts all people, even if they don't believe in Him, as long as they were good people.

I don't know if this is true or not – I'm no theologian – but the Bible says, 'Whoever so believes in me….' I think there must be some compensation for good people because the Bible also says God is forgiving. It's all too confusing for me; I just know there is a God.

We all know plenty of good people that don't go to church. Obviously church isn't necessary for all people to be good, but it sure helps. I look at God like the analogy I made about love: you need to water it. Prayer is the water to help the love for God to grow. Bible study is part of the water, but so are acts of kindness, volunteerism, helping those less fortunate… So you can get by without prayer and church attendance, but it's more difficult. Without water, the love for God is in danger of withering and dying and so, too, a life fulfilled.

I love life. I did before, but in knowing God it is even grander, despite my wheelchair.

* * *

Love acted as a buoy, preventing me from sinking in despair, but it didn't prevent me from feeling despair. I acknowledged that the drug experiment had failed and that I was a prisoner of my muscle tone. My muscles seemed willing to relearn but rigidity held them back.

Todd, my roommate, was discharged in early March. Underneath his youthful bravado there was a very kind and gentle soul. I was going to miss him. He left quietly without fanfare while I ate my lunch in the cafeteria. It was typical of Todd: accepting fate with little fuss. He would not want to be the centre of attention.

My discharge date – the end of March – held firm. I was eager to start my new life at home. Each attempt at walking became a disappointment for me. Each failed attempt at sitting or standing only drove home the point to me: it was time to go home.

I would receive physical therapy at home and I felt I was more likely to make gains attempting the functional activities of daily living at home.

I had daydreamed of walking out of Stan Cassidy on my discharge date: I would have a walker; my gait would be wobbly, my legs dancing with muscle clonus, but I'd be walking independently. I'd walk from my room, down the corridor, and stop at the front desk. There I'd wait while Jill brought the car to the front door. While waiting, I'd joke with Laura, the receptionist at the front desk, about her upcoming wedding. She'd remark at how good it was to see me walk. I'd thank her for saying so. The car would arrive about then and I'd walk out the front door and into my car. It wasn't going to happen.

My secret dream of walking out of Stan Cassidy was not going to be fulfilled. It hurt but I had had months to reconcile myself to reality. Like all things in life: when you hit a wall – back up and go around. It was my time to try another avenue.

I decided to accept my failure for now, but that didn't mean I would never walk. *I will keep trying. I might.* I was back to the possibilities.

I wrote a short note to each nurse, nursing assistant, doctor, and therapist, as a thank you. Nearly a year of my life had been spent in Stan Cassidy and I owed them so much. I had taken from each a part of their personality they had to offer. From some I took their humour, some their smile, advice, sincerity, or kindness. They had helped me remain focused on life.

I thought back to those days of being 'locked in' – dark, ugly days brightened by smiles, jokes, hugs. I had so much to be grateful for. I had come through a tunnel so narrow that my thoughts seemed imprisoned. Each nurse, assistant, doctor, and therapist was instrumental in pulling me through.

I had become dependent upon my therapists, especially Mereille. I came to think of Mereille as my angel, a light to help me through these difficult times. And perhaps that is what angels are: people we don't expect who come forward and guide us through difficult times.

Mereille cried when I said farewell and thanked her for all she had done. I didn't cry. I was finally in command of my emotions – though I'm not saying that is a good thing. It was time to go and I broke easily away from Mereille, Doreen, Beth, and Tracey.

It felt odd to look back at Stan Cassidy as we drove away. The little white cement building had embraced the greatest struggle of my life. It seemed unfair to be just leaving it without fanfare, quiet as we turned left out the driveway, up the hill. I left behind some fears but also some hopes and dreams.

I was reflective as we drove home. Life has changed for me – leaving Stan Cassidy gave me a final perspective: I will never, ever be the same. I had thought I would become an agile old fellow, bouncing grandchildren on my knee. I'd have a penchant for plaid, flannel shirts, and jeans. I'd be up early, doing odd jobs before breakfast. I'd still be canoeing, sailing, and doing manual labour into my seventies. I'd show my grandchildren how to hammer a nail. I'd take them on hikes into the wood. All gone.

I had to remind myself Jill was beside me – what more did I want? I'd shift my focus – my ambitions in life. Still I couldn't rally out of the doldrums. It should have been a happy day – a day I had been dreaming about. Instead my thoughts clouded my mood and I remained sullen.

Reality set in as I drove up to my home. This is my home.

This is my life. I pivoted out of my car with Jill's help, realizing that this was only a new beginning. Life would be different but that didn't exclude fun, laughter, and love.

Jill wheeled me up the ramp and around to my back door. When I opened the door, my face broke into a grin I hope never fades – my children had decorated the kitchen with one hundred different coloured balloons. It was magical. I was home.

EPILOGUE

I was most interested in the physical outcomes of brainstem stroke survivors as I read their stories. I suppose I was looking for some hope, but what I found I didn't like. Outcomes were varied: some walked, others didn't; some stayed locked in, others were given a key. But there seemed to be one constant: the function attained in the first year seemed to be the best function attained. Improvements were made after one year, but they made little impact on the overall function.

I was wrong – function can improve. I started physical, occupational, and speech therapy as an outpatient at the Saint John Regional Hospital. I went three times a week. Two years later I am now going once a week and going to a private gym twice a week.

I have been blessed with the involvement of many lovely and caring therapists. Cathy Belding, Irene Thompson, and Marlene Wowchuk have been my Physical Therapists. My Occupational Therapists have been Marla Scichilone and Dawn Hunter, and my Speech Language Pathologist has been Charlotte Polley.

They have different approaches, different results, and different failures. I keep an open mind and try different techniques. Some Physical Therapists use a Neurological Developmental Training method (NDT), others use more traditional methods, and most use a combination.

I found NDT methods more effective but not necessarily so. Putting body weight on my affected right arm is supposed to decrease tone and then increase function: it never worked for me. It did decrease my tone but it was not long lasting. That is not to say it wouldn't work for you.

I never found working my legs in slings effective. Any gain I might have attained did not translate to function. Stair work did help function in stepping.

I am not delving any farther into what technique helped me and what didn't – it would be too technical. Each therapist worked hard in trying to help me and for that I am very grateful. I gained something from everyone.

It has not been easy; it is hard to stay motivated when the exercises get monotonous and no or little reward is obtained. But it is worth it.

Every morning Jill stretches my limbs; three times a week a nursing assistant, Doug Conway, does the task. I see this will probably have to be a daily routine for the rest of my life. I would be stiff and contracted without the stretches. My hope is that the time spent on the exercises will be reduced.

My speech has been a pleasant surprise; it is now two and a half years since my stroke and my speech is still improving. Four months ago no one could understand my phone conversations: now I phone people regularly. I cannot emphasise enough how slow the improvement is, but it is occurring. So don't give up!

I practice holding a note, making my voice slide from low pitch to high pitch and vice versa, and singing. It's boring (except for the singing), unrewarding (unless you look back over time), but so necessary. I will never have a normal voice, but I'm aiming to be close after years of work.

I eat better. I still tend to chew with the front teeth – my tongue has a hard time moving any food over to the side teeth, but it's improving. I couldn't chew gum four months ago – now I can.

I can drink anything but I have to be careful with clear fluids – small amounts and tuck my chin in. I forget, look up to see someone or something, and choke. I'm used to choking and so I tell visitors: "Don't be alarmed if I choke. Please don't perform the Heimlich Manoeuvre unless I turn blue." So far, thankfully, the Heimlich has never been needed.

My body is stiff; it balks at allowing me to turn or bend. My balance is poor but better. My left arm is quite functional – I typed this account with it – but has trouble extending and reaching for things. My right arm is stubborn; it wants to stay close to my body with the elbow bent and my hand in my lap. When I can think of it, I fight this tendency.

My right hand wanted to stay contracted like a claw. It has improved just lately; it is more relaxed. I can hold a utensil and with difficulty, eat; I can hold a pencil and I write, before tone kicks in. I attribute this success to the use of botulism toxin or Botox.

This neurotoxin is derived from the bacteria responsible for botulism that produces a severe form of food poisoning. Botulism may result in death by paralysis. This neurotoxin that causes the paralysis is not harmful if injected into a targeted muscle; it does not disseminate throughout the body.

My biceps muscle is constantly 'on', leaving me with a bent elbow. My triceps muscle (the muscle in back of the upper arm) is not strong enough to overcome the strength of the biceps, and thus allow me to extend the arm. By relaxing the biceps with the toxin, the triceps is given a chance to strengthen, and the biceps can be stretched.

The toxin paralysis lasts about three months, and hopefully, when the rigidity returns, it won't be as tight as the opposing muscle will be stronger. The paralysis induced isn't total but only relaxes the muscle. I have been happy with the results.

I attribute to the use of Botox improvement in my right arm and hand, but what about my legs?

I bought a power chair after I came home; or I should say my insurance company bought it for me, on recommendation of Marla, my Occupational Therapist. It took me awhile to accept this into my life. My attempt at walking had failed – as did using a manual chair; my right arm never became good enough. While accepting a power chair admitted defeat, it also gave me independence. I also realized it didn't have to be a permanent defeat. I can still try to walk. I considered the chair a convenience; it was reality – a setback, a retreat – not a defeat.

The power chair, besides giving me much more independence, is comfortable. I remember when I couldn't conceive of spending the rest of my days in a chair and I wrestled with the feeling of being trapped in a wheelchair; I had to get out. I still sit on a sofa for a change but I much prefer my chair. It is more comfortable, and the irony is: I'm actually trapped on the sofa.

My secret ambition was still to walk. Mereille, I knew, still held out hope for me, and my new therapists still took me for 'walks', but I was a sad study in gait form. I didn't verbalize my desires too strenuously to my therapists: I didn't want the pressure. Every night, however, I prayed for the strength to continue.

Tara, my youngest child, was often the only one home to help me. Colin and Beth helped when they were home from university, but mainly it was Tara. Every night she would stand in front of the walker, to prevent it from going forward too fast and also to help place my feet.

Jill stood behind me holding my right hand on the walker, steadying me, and pushing my legs forward as though I were stepping. We went from my kitchen to living room – night after night.

I came home in April 2000 and we persevered for over a year: night after night, the same unrewarding procedure. I feared my dream was a dream – never to be fulfilled. I would like to tell you, I said I was determined to succeed or I wouldn't give up – and other such noble statements. But it was fear really. I feared giving up. I feared failure.

I felt my obstacle to walking was my rigidity. My muscles behind my upper legs (hamstrings) and the muscles that pulled my legs together were too tight. If they could be relaxed, I might walk. It was then that Dr. Milczarek told me about a new procedure that was becoming available: Botox injections.

In the meantime, I had to keep trying – trying to break the tone on my own. The more effort I put into lifting and bending my knee, the greater my tone became. Frustrated, hopeless at times, I kept banging into this wall of failure. The only path around it that I saw, lay with the medical procedures. This time I couldn't back up and go around: I would have to wait. Meanwhile, I kept banging at that darn wall.

Jill was always behind me, emotionally and physically, my safety net. She wouldn't let me quit. It was physically challenging for her: holding my hand on the walker while pushing my feet ahead with her legs, and watching my balance. Pushing my feet ahead was an exhausting exercise because of the rigidity in my legs, but she never complained or took a night off. She was often the one who reminded me that it was time to try my walk.

Love helped me get through the dark days and love still helps me; encourages me to continue. Love is still my safety net and the staff I lean on.

Botox eventually came into common use and Dr. Milczarek gave me a small dose in September of 2000. It relaxed my legs and relieved the pain I was experiencing in my hamstrings. I could stretch them farther but this translated into little improvement in function at first. My arm and shoulder got injected also – December, March, and June 2001.

I broke the tone in my legs sometime during this period – at first very slowly, then faster. I moved my foot a little past the other foot; it became easier for Jill to push my leg through. Remember no eurekas.

June. The dose in June did it! I moved my leg past the other – far ahead of the other. All by myself! It started out with one step, one leg, then the next time I took two steps by myself. Soon I was walking with only Jill, back and forth from my kitchen to living room.

I am walking.

It is not pretty, nor am I independent, but it's a start.

It has taken me over two years, but my dream is fulfilled. So don't give up. Be ready to accept but not without a good try.

Sometimes progress is not possible – for a while – but there are always new breakthroughs in treatments and research.

Now that I am walking some, I plan to get my right wrist stronger, so that I can hold the walker by myself. Then I'm going to learn to stand by myself. Finally, I'll be independent enough to stand, grab my walker, and walk to my next destination. Then maybe quad canes instead of a walker; then maybe...

This will take years and a lot of work, but I have a plan and Love to sustain me, and a dream to reach for – never, ever, give up on your dreams.

ABOUT THE AUTHOR

Dr. Shawn Jennings was born and grew up in Saint John, New Brunswick. After Saint John High School, he attended Dalhousie University in Halifax, receiving his B.Sc. in 1974. He then went on to Dalhousie Medical School, receiving his MD in 1978. After a rotating internship throughout the Maritimes, he began a practice of Family Medicine in Saint John in 1979. He enjoyed his life as a Family Doctor in Saint John for twenty years, ending with a brainstem stroke in 1999. He has resided for many years in the Town of Rothesay, where he lives still with his wife Jill and their three children, Colin, Beth, and Tara.